T0162580

Facing Our Mortality Without Fear:
Advice From The Great Philosophers

Facing Our Mortality Without Fear: Advice From The Great Philosophers

ROBERT BONSER

iUniverse, Inc.
Bloomington

Facing Our Mortality Without Fear: Advice From The Great
Philosophers

Copyright © 2011 by Robert Bonser.

All rights reserved. No part of this book may be used or reproduced by any means, graphic, electronic, or mechanical, including photocopying, recording, taping or by any information storage retrieval system without the written permission of the publisher except in the case of brief quotations embodied in critical articles and reviews.

iUniverse books may be ordered through booksellers or by contacting:

iUniverse
1663 Liberty Drive
Bloomington, IN 47403
www.iuniverse.com
1-800-Authors (1-800-288-4677)

Because of the dynamic nature of the Internet, any web addresses or links contained in this book may have changed since publication and may no longer be valid. The views expressed in this work are solely those of the author and do not necessarily reflect the views of the publisher, and the publisher hereby disclaims any responsibility for them.

Any people depicted in stock imagery provided by Thinkstock are models, and such images are being used for illustrative purposes only.
Certain stock imagery © Thinkstock.

ISBN: 978-1-4620-3399-7 (sc)
ISBN: 978-1-4620-3400-0 (ebk)

Printed in the United States of America

iUniverse rev. date: 07/19/2011

To my wife, Wen

CONTENTS

INTRODUCTION

The general theme of this book is the relationship of philosophy to death, that is, to an awareness of our own mortality. This theme is an ancient one, going all the way back to Plato, who, in the *Phaedo* has Socrates tell us that philosophy is "preparation" or "practice" for death. There is a proud tradition in philosophy of being able to offer consolation and comfort for all of the trials and tribulations of life, including the greatest and final trial—death. Since Plato's time the subject of how the practice of philosophy might help us to overcome the fear of death has been taken up by many thinkers, among them, quite notably, the French philosopher, Montaigne. Montaigne, himself, borrows heavily from others, such as Socrates, Cicero, and Seneca.

Death may seem like a morbid subject to write upon, but one of the first things the philosopher notices when turning his attention to understanding life is that there is something off to the side, in his peripheral vision that demands attention, namely that life has an end to it. In other words, it is impossible to hope for any true insight into life without also including death in our purview. The opposite is also true: that it is nearly impossible to understand death in any meaningful way without also examining our lives.

The book as a whole is loosely organized around Socrates' claim in the *Apology* that: "Death is one of two things. Either it is annihilation, and the dead have no consciousness of anything, or, as we are told, it is really a change—a migration of the soul from this place to another."[1] This observation in itself might not seem particularly profound, except that Socrates goes on to say that *either way* death is not something to be feared, and can even be seen as a positive good. Part One will focus primarily on the fear of death when regarded as extinction, and Part Two on the possibility of an afterlife. In Part One we'll examine Montaigne's writings on death as a way of approaching the subject, along with the views of many other philosophers. Montaigne is a good candidate to take us on this journey, since many commentators regard him as a thorough skeptic.

And in Part Two, we'll consider Socrates' second possibility—that the soul persists in some way, and how it may be possible from a philosophical standpoint to make sense of this. One might think that to say that there is an afterlife is enough to remove the fear of death, but in truth, many religious visions of the hereafter are not entirely comforting. Christianity and Islam particularly present us with the possibility of a hellish afterlife, and some Buddhist texts, like the *Tibetan Book of the Dead*, populate the afterlife with demons. But are such models philosophically coherent? We'll look at this question and ultimately suggest an alternative vision of the afterlife.

The ancient Greeks were not afraid of the subject, and Socrates, in the *Phaedo*, goes on at length to describe his version of the afterlife, even providing a kind of "geography" of heaven. Possibly because Plato and Socrates sought to explore those things "most needful" in life, such as truth, goodness, love, and beauty, they recognized the need to at least consider whether there is an afterlife and what it might be like. Plato, especially, taught that it isn't just that we desire to possess the highest things, but we desire to possess them forever. Thus the wish for immortality is built-in to our other desires.

The question of the immortality of the soul, after all, has an enormous impact on the things we come to regard as most important in life. Truth, goodness, and beauty suddenly become desperately poignant if they are confined to the brief span of a human life, only to be followed by the oblivion of death. It may be true that they come to be held as more precious in being so fleeting, but at the same time they come perilously close to being engulfed in meaninglessness in the absence of an afterlife. In other words, death not only ends our life but seems to devalue it as well.

In any case, I believe it is a worthy philosophical question to inquire as to what sort of afterlife would most make sense of our earthly lives. To this question, at least, reason can be applied. Rather than listening to congregations of angels sing *Allelieua* or staring into the face of God for eternity, what might we actually *do* there? What would lend the most meaning to our former earthly life? What becomes of such concepts as justice, mercy, forgiveness, truth, goodness, and beauty when we try to formulate a sensible heaven? I try to explore this from the standpoint of philosophy rather than religion. This is true in a double-sense—not only to examine the afterlife from the perspective of reason rather than revelation, but also to suggest that philosophy or the "love of wisdom" may itself have something to do with what occupies us in the hereafter, and that it is eminently reasonable that this should be the case.

Mark Twain once observed how odd it is that the pursuit of truth never figures into man's conception of heaven. "It is curious, it is noteworthy, that no heaven has ever been offered him wherein his one sole superiority was provided with a chance to enjoy itself. Even when he himself has imagined a heaven, he has never made provision in it for intellectual joys. It is a striking omission."[2] This is an omission which I try to remedy.

Beyond this, it was also my hope to try to offer a kind of reassuring "meditation" upon our mortality. I've heard that for Tibetan Buddhists the *Book of the Dead* is read aloud at the time of death with the purpose of guiding the deceased through the various phases of the afterlife. My own wish here would be to provide a meditation for those troubled by thoughts of death, a sort of guide to navigate our minds and souls to a more hopeful and tranquil state.

PART ONE

MONTAIGNE ON THE FEAR OF DEATH

Chapter 1

Know Your Adversary

Most people have probably heard of Woody Allen's quip that he isn't afraid of death—he just doesn't want to be there when it happens. My own guess is that what people are most afraid of is not so much that they'll be there when it happens, but that after it happens, they'll no longer be anywhere. In truth, the fear of death takes many forms: the fear of non-being, the fear that it will be painful, the fear of the unknown, the fear of punishment in the afterlife, the regrets of unfinished business, the fear of leaving behind loved ones who need our care, and so on.

What do we do about these fears? As indicated in the introduction, there is a tradition in philosophy which has sought to provide an answer. Philosophy is essentially the search for truth, or the "love of wisdom," *philia* (love) and *sophos* (wisdom). Probably the most central fear of death is the fear of the unknown. How will we die? Will it be painful? When will we die? Is there an afterlife? And so on. The best antidote to the fear of the unknown, of course, is knowledge. Granted that there is a veil between life and death so that we may never have full knowledge until we experience it directly, nevertheless, by approaching the subject from every angle, seeking the truth about it, and most of all, looking at it unflinchingly, we can begin to diminish our fears.

One of the best examples of a philosopher taking this approach is Michel de Montaigne, a French philosopher of the sixteenth century. Over his lifetime Montaigne recorded his thoughts on every conceivable subject from "Of the greatness of Rome," to "Of thumbs." He wrote of the great and sublime as well as the petty and profane. His collected *Essays* run to 857 pages. But it quickly becomes clear to anyone reading these essays that one of the subjects most on his mind is death. Montaigne himself confesses: "Since my earliest days, there is nothing with which

I have occupied my mind more than with images of death."[3] Over ten percent of the 107 articles in the *Essays* take up this subject.

Montaigne was aware, however, that even the mention of death may make people anxious. Some people, he tells us, "take fright at the mere mention of death, and most of them cross themselves at the mention of that name, as at the name of the devil . . . Because this syllable struck their ears too harshly and seemed to them unlucky, the Romans learned to soften it or to spread it out in a periphrasis. Instead of saying, 'He is dead,' they say, 'He has ceased to live,' or 'He has lived.' Provided it is life, even past, they take comfort. We have borrowed from them our, 'late Mr. Jones.'"[4]

In America, of course, we have many euphemisms for death: "pass away," "cross over," "croak," "buy the farm," "kick the bucket," bite the dust," "give up the ghost," and many more. If these euphemisms are slightly humorous or whimsical, all the better to take the sting out. One contemporary humorist writes of the endless euphemisms invented to soften the harshness of some of the vocabulary associated with death. An undertaker becomes a "funeral director," the dead person is the "decedent," a funeral becomes a "memorial service," the corpse or dead body is the "earthly remains," and a grave is a "final resting place."[5]

From the beginning of his reflections upon death, Montaigne raises the question whether it's really true that people are so terrified at the thought of death. Considering how easily and readily people face it, we may tend to exaggerate the presence of this fear. While stories of famous men and women facing death bravely inspire all of us, accounts of less exalted, normal people behaving courageously in similar circumstances are not hard to find. To begin with, millions have faced death bravely in wars, fighting for their countries and families, and often in the name of higher political ideals. Religious beliefs, certainly, have produced many who have been willing to martyr themselves for their beliefs. Mothers have willingly sacrificed their lives for their children. People have voluntarily gone to death for honor, glory, love, country, family, and so forth. Montaigne writes: "If I were to string together here a long list of those of all sexes and conditions and sects who have either awaited death resolutely or sought it voluntarily, and sought it not only to flee the ills of this life, but some simply to flee satiety with living and others for the hope of a better condition elsewhere, I should never be done."[6]

In other words, there are many things that people attach more value to than life itself. Death is not the highest fear. The thought of harm coming to our loved ones frightens us more. Some may feel that not having the courage of their convictions is worse than death. There is even a survey showing that the fear of public speaking ranked higher than the fear of death. This sounds a little ingenuous to me, although I suppose if we interpret "public speaking" as making ourselves susceptible to the possibility of public humiliation, then it may actually be true. As one wit has observed, though, if this were really true, it would mean that when such people attended a funeral, they'd rather be in the casket than have to deliver the eulogy. In any case, Montaigne is aware that however the fear of death is ranked alongside our other fears, it is very real.

If the goal is to overcome the fear of death, as it is for Montaigne, we might begin by asking whether we are really more likely to do so by focusing our attention fully upon our mortality, or rather, simply try to ignore it and go our merry way through life? There are some who suggest that if we obsess too much about death, we'll undermine any real chance of enjoying our lives. Epicurus, for example, advised us to simply displace negative thoughts with happy memories from our past and anticipations of future pleasures.

To some extent, modern society encourages us to become preoccupied with death. Death, for instance, appears to be the archenemy of "progress." How can the American Dream and the Good Life include death? Death comes to be seen almost as a kind of failure or an "insult," a final slap in the face. Thus, in our society death is often regarded as just another disease to be conquered by science and technology.

Montaigne himself apparently changed his view over time on whether we will benefit more by turning our attention toward or away from our mortality. In his early essays he clearly believes that the more we meditate on our mortality, the easier it will be to meet death without fear. In his essay, "That to philosophize is to learn to die," it is his opinion that the most frightening thing about death is our fear of the unknown. The solution would seem to be then to direct our gaze toward it and come to know it as best we're able. "Let us rid it of its strangeness, come to know it, get used to it. Let us have nothing on our minds as often as death, at every moment let us picture it in all its aspects . . . It is uncertain where death awaits us; let us await it everywhere. Premeditation of death is premeditation of freedom. He who has learned how to die has unlearned how to be a slave."[7]

Montaigne may have borrowed this thought from the Stoic philosopher and Roman Emperor, Marcus Aurelius, who wrote in his *Meditations*, "We should apprehend, too, the nature of death; and that if only it be steadily contemplated, and the fancies we associate with it be mentally dissected, it will soon come to be thought of as no more than a process of nature."[8]

We can see the truth of this, sometimes, from our own experience. When a loved one, such as a parent, goes through a protracted illness before passing away, we often grow slightly more accustomed to the idea of their passing from being led to repeatedly reflect on it and imagine it in our mind. The same sort of thing might be applied to ourselves. We may find that by reflecting upon our own mortality, by mentally rehearsing it, the though will gradually lose some of its sting. Montaigne, here, heavily under the influence of the Stoics, is following their advice on how to best meet the unpredictability of fortune.

Cicero, the Roman philosopher and orator, and one of Montaigne's favorites, recalls the story of the philosopher, Anaxagorus, who when told that his son had died, accepted the news calmly. When asked why he wasn't more shocked and upset, he responded, "I knew that I had begotten a mortal." Cicero goes on to tell us, "This saying shows that such events are cruel for those who have not reflected on them. Therefore it does not admit of doubt that everything which is thought evil is more grievous if it comes unexpectedly. And so . . . as foresight and anticipation have considerable effect in lessening pain, a human being should ponder all the vicissitudes that fall to man's lot."[9] The goal is to understand and continually remind ourselves of the unpredictability of fortune. Today we're rich, tomorrow we may be poor; today healthy, tomorrow ill; today happily married, tomorrow divorced; and on and on. The same approach should be employed with respect to our own mortality. The Stoics believed that the most painful aspect of any misfortune is often its unexpectedness. The shock from this unexpectedness provides most of the pain involved, and can be greatly alleviated simply by anticipation. This includes the anticipation and mental rehearsal of the ongoing possibility of death.

Montaigne, then, at least in his early writings, felt it was useful to occupy himself with an awareness of death. He tells us that he was assisted in this, beginning in middle age, by an ailment he had apparently inherited from his father—kidney stones. This malady plagued him until the end of his life, though ultimately it was not what killed him. It served the purpose, though, of making him more intimately acquainted with his own mortality. Montaigne records that because of stones he would sometimes be unable to pass urine for as long as three days, bringing him close to death. "I have at least this profit from the stone, that it will complete what I have still not been able to accomplish in myself and reconcile and familiarize me completely with death; for the more my illness oppresses and bothers me, the less will death be something for me to fear. I had already accomplished this: to hold to life by life alone. My illness will undo even this bond; and God grant that in the end, if its sharpness comes to surpass my powers, it may not throw me back to the other extreme, which is no less a vice, of loving and desiring to die."[10]

What does Montaigne mean when he says that he had already learned to hold on to life by life alone? In another essay, it's made clear that he believed he had met all of his family obligations and need not worry about their welfare if he should pass away. "Death often weighs heavier on us by its weight on others, and pains us by their pain almost as much as by our own, and sometimes even more,"[11] he writes. This sort of consideration plagues many of us when contemplating our own passing. How will our family get by without us? Are they financially secure? Are the children's future on track? Will they become good people without our guidance? But Montaigne did not have these worries. He had fathered five daughters, but only one, now an adult, survived, and he knew that she would be adequately provided for. He felt he had reached the point in life where his death would "give scarcely any pleasure or displeasure to anyone."[12]

He had no unfinished projects. When he wrote this he was in retirement from public life and his *Essays* were essentially completed. Hence the only thing still attaching him to life was life itself, that is, whatever pleasure came from simply being alive. And now with the agony of kidney stones the pain was beginning to outweigh the pleasure. It was this ailment, he admits, which really began to acquaint him with his own mortality, rather than his continued musings on death throughout his life. What before was an exercise of the imagination now became a painful reality. Indeed, by the latter part of his life he had concluded that such philosophizing actually tended to undercut any real enjoyment of life. "Of what use to us is this curiosity to anticipate all the ills of life, and prepare ourselves with so much trouble to encounter even those which are perhaps never to touch us? . . . On the contrary, the easiest and most natural thing would be to unburden even our thoughts of them. Apparently they will not come soon enough; our mind must extend and prolong them, incorporate them into itself and dwell on them beforehand, as if they did not weigh reasonably upon our senses."[13] Montaigne quotes Seneca, another Roman philosopher and statesman, who advises us that such misfortunes "will weigh heavily enough when they are upon us. Meanwhile favor yourself; believe what you like best. What good does it do you to welcome and anticipate your bad fortune, to lose the present through fear of the future, and to be miserable now because you are to be so in time?"[14]

Rather than following Plato's teaching that philosophy prepares us for death, Montaigne concluded, in a reversal of his earlier view, that it can be dispensed with altogether. Nature takes care of such matters without the help of philosophy. "It is certain," he declares, "that to most people preparation for death has given more torment than the dying . . . If you don't know how to die, don't worry, Nature will tell you what to do on the spot, fully and adequately. She will do this job perfectly for you; don't bother your head about it."[15] Or as someone once said, death is easy. It's living that's hard.

And what is it that Nature tells us when we're close to death? In his essays, Montaigne recounts a traumatic experience that put him at death's door. While out riding in the country with friends, another horse and rider came around the corner at full-speed, smashing head-on into him and his horse. Montaigne was flung far from his horse and knocked senseless. Thinking him near death, his friends carried him toward home. Along the way, he was semi-conscious and threw up tremendous quantities of blood from internal bleeding. He tells it this way: "Meanwhile my condition was, in truth, very pleasant and peaceful. I felt no affliction either for others or for myself; it was a languor and an extreme weakness, without any pain. I saw my house without recognizing it. When they had put me to bed, I felt infinite sweetness in this repose . . . They offered me many remedies, of which I accepted none, holding it for certain that I was mortally wounded in the head. It would, in truth, have been a very happy death, for the weakness of my understanding kept me from having any judgment of it, and that of my body from having any feeling of it. I was letting myself slip away so gently, so gradually and easily, that I hardly ever did anything with less of a feeling of effort."[16]

Over a period of days, Montaigne recovered but found the experience to be instructive, writing that, "in truth, in order to get used to the idea of death, I find that there is nothing like coming close to it."[17] Montaigne's account reminds me of H. L. Mencken's description in his essay, "Exeunt Omnes:" "All the authorities, it is pleasant to know, report that the final scene is commonly devoid of terror. The dying man doesn't struggle much and he isn't much afraid. As the body gives out he succumbs to a blest stupidity. His mind fogs. His will power vanishes. He submits decently. He scarcely gives a damn."[18] In other words, Nature stupefies us. Nearing death, our body pumps us full of endorphins, a natural sedative, so that we might meet our end blissfully.

I think it is interesting that this is virtually the opposite of what we might expect of nature. It seems far more likely that nature would pump high levels of adrenalin into our system to increase the chances of survival, rather than sedate or pacify us to the acceptance of death. What natural purpose could it serve to have us "feel good" about death? Why should nature be merciful in these last moments? It is very much as if nature were trying to tell us something:—there's nothing to be afraid of.

It appears, then, that if our goal is to complete a list of ways in which we might learn to overcome the fear of death, Montaigne, in the evolution of his thought, actually offers us two opposing approaches.

1. Through anticipation and mental rehearsal we can become more accustomed to an awareness of our own mortality and thereby less afraid;
2. We should ignore and avoid thoughts of death as such thoughts will only undermine enjoyment of life. Nature will guide us when the time comes.

Which Montaigne is correct? Montaigne the Stoic or Montaigne the naturalist? This, of course, is up to everyone to decide for themselves, but if I were to weigh in on the subject, I'd say that even though the natural tendency of people may be to avoid thoughts of death, for most it's not really possible. It's often said that since animals have little or no awareness of their own mortality, they have no ongoing fear of death other than the momentary response of instinct when being attacked. Otherwise, for those animals who grow old, death is met with equanimity. They fall ill, lie down, fall into unconsciousness, and pass away without all of the fears of anticipation. Perhaps this is why we say that the happiest of human deaths is when we die peacefully in our sleep—going to bed, not knowing that we won't wake up the next morning. Montaigne observes that, "Caesar, when they asked him what death he found most desirable, answered: 'The least premeditated and the quickest.' If Caesar dared say it," Montaigne continues, "It is no longer cowardice for me to believe it."[19]

But is it really possible for humans to ignore their own mortality? Animals can do so because they are more or less suspended in time with very little memory of the past and virtually no awareness of the future. For most people, it would be difficult to approach life in this way. First of all, it is nearly impossible to not be mindful of our own mortality when we see so many others dying around us—grandparents, parents, siblings, friends, and worst of all, sometimes our own children. And now, with modern news media reporting death and destruction around the world each day, it becomes nearly impossible to avert our eyes. To do so would be like the proverbial ostrich burying his head in the sand—not a very philosophical image. The more important question is how should we respond once we have this awareness? We can try to push it to the back of our mind if we choose, but this may be more likely to create a vague and generalized sense of unease.

Much better to do as some of the Stoics suggested, and as Montaigne originally advised, and rather than trying to avert our attention, look the matter square-on. If we are to have any chance of finding meaning in our own mortality, and if we value truth, then it is best that we don't try to look away. If anything, as we grow older, the grief we experience in the passing of so many people we have cared about is more likely to diminish our attachment to life, and even perhaps make us long to join them on the other side. In this case death begins to seem like going home. It could even be said that grieving at the loss of others is at least one way in which nature begins to detach us emotionally from life and prepare us for death, or even make us long for it.

The Stoics did not wish that we should obsess about death, but only that we should try to calmly consider it as well as we're able. Instead of undercutting the enjoyment of life, it may actually enhance our enjoyment. And what is more likely to make us appreciate life than when we have a near brush with death? Those who survive serious illnesses, automobile accidents, and a multitude of other calamities, nearly always come to appreciate the preciousness of life all the more and the importance of living each day to the fullest. All in all, then, I tend to agree with Montaigne's earlier view that it is useful, in overcoming the fear of death, to seek to have some familiarity and knowledge of it to the extent we're able.

If it were true that death is extinction, it would signify the end of all pain and therefore be nothing to fear. But the fact that the fear remains tells us that it is the fear itself which is the problem. In other words, death is not a problem for the dead, but only for the living. In our fear we "die a thousand deaths." The goal then is to begin to detach or distance ourselves from our fear.

The approach of philosophy in seeking to diminish the force of sometimes debilitating emotions is to examine them as objectively as possible. During the time that we're analyzing our emotions, whether it's fear or anger or sadness, we are one step removed from them. The subjective becomes objective. The focus shifts from emotion to intellect, from feeling to understanding. But beyond this simple detachment, we can also benefit when we come to see that at least some part of the emotion may be irrational. Phobias, for example, are considered to be irrational fears, but we may discover, at a deeper level, that nearly all fears have a large irrational component.

In analyzing our emotions, they are transfigured into the category of "the interesting." They occupy our intellect rather than our feelings. They are puzzles to be solved, not passions to be endured. This is actually a process of self-discovery or self-knowledge. This isn't to say that there is nothing to be learned from emotions, only that we should try to discern that part which is real and true from that which is fanciful and unfounded.

It was Socrates, at the beginning of the Western tradition, who taught that the ultimate goal of philosophy is self-knowledge—to "know thyself." And of all the emotions it is fear which presents the greatest obstacle to such knowledge. Fear may turn many people to superstition and harmful beliefs. Or it may lead to an obsession with other unworthy substitutes such as greed for wealth or desire for fame and glory. Much of our "quiet desperation" in life may be tied to the fear of death, often at an unconscious level. The more we're able to look squarely at the fact of our own mortality, without flinching, and examine our fears from the broadest possible perspective, this fear will be dissipated.

Chapter 2

Nature's Way

One of Montaigne's central arguments for why death should not be feared is that it is natural. This, no doubt, requires a certain amount of faith that Nature itself is "good." I think this faith is justified and we'll talk more about this later, but meanwhile we can see that as we become less attached to life, we become less fearful of death. This happens in a few different ways. First of all, life itself acquaints us with death. Not only in the sense of experiencing the death of others around us, but also in the natural process of growing old. As we grow older, the illnesses and infirmities of age make us more aware of our mortality and prepare us gradually to accept it as a release. With respect to his own experience, Montaigne states, "I notice that in proportion as I sink into sickness, I naturally enter into a certain disdain for life . . . When we are led by Nature's hand down a gentle and virtually imperceptible slope, bit by bit, one step at a time, she rolls us into this wretched state and makes us familiar with it, so that we feel no shock when youth dies within us."[20]

Or perhaps with a more humorous slant, Emerson bemoans old age this way: "'Tis strange that it is not in vogue to commit hari-kari, as the Japanese do. Nature is so insulting in her hints and notices, does not pull you by the sleeve, but pulls out your teeth, tears off your hair in patches, steals your eyesight, twists your face into an ugly mask, in short, puts all contumelies upon you, without in the least abating your zeal to make a good appearance, and all this at the same time that she is moulding the new figures around you into wonderful beauty which of course is only making your plight worse."[21]

Beyond the wear and tear of aging, our attachment to life is diminished in other ways as we advance with age. In our later years many of our goals have been accomplished or set aside. Perhaps we have worked hard all our life, raised a family, achieved some level of material comfort and security.

These things no longer continue to occupy us in the same way. According to Montaigne, "for as much as I no longer cling so hard to the good things of life when I begin to lose the use and pleasure of them, I come to view death with much less frightened eyes. This makes me hope that the farther I get from life and the nearer to death, the more easily I shall accept the exchange."[22]

Those who make it to advanced age may find that many of their former desires have abated, including sexual desire. Yet, this frees us from one more of the "ties that bind." It's fascinating that the most famous philosophical work ever written, Plato's *Republic*, begins with two old men discussing the loss of sexual fervor. The elderly Cephalus tells of hearing someone ask the Greek poet Sophocles, also advanced in age, "How about your service to Aphrodite, Sophocles—is your natural force still unabated? And he replied, 'Hush, man, most gladly have I escaped this thing you talk of, as if I had run away from a raging and savage beast of a master.'" Cephalus comments, "I thought it a good answer then and now I think so still more. For in very truth there comes to old age a great tranquility in such matters and a blessed release."[23]

And what applies to sexual desire applies to other desires. Seneca in his old age rejoiced, "How sweet it is to have outworn desires and left them behind."[24] And Cicero in his essay, "On Old Age," writes, "The objection is that old people are no longer tickled by their senses. I agree—but they do not want to be either! . . . Covet such things, and the lack of them may well be tiresome and annoying, but it you have had enough of them and are replete, to lack becomes more pleasant than to possess! Or rather, if you do not miss their absence, you cannot be said to lack them."[25]

Every stage in life has its own interests and activities. Childhood, adolescence, adulthood, and old age all have their characteristic pursuits. But "One has had enough of life," Cicero declares, "when one has had enough of all its occupations."[26] Cicero, once again, observes, "In the same way as apples, when green, can only be picked by force, but after ripening to maturity fall of by themselves, so death comes to the young with violence, but to old people when the time is ripe. And the thought of this ripeness so greatly attracts me that as I approach death I feel like a man nearing harbor after a long voyage; I seem to be catching sight of land."[27] And Milton, who may have read Cicero's essay, wrote, "So may'st thou live, till, like ripe fruit thou drop / Into thy mother's lap, or be with ease / Gathered, not harshly plucked, for death mature: / This is old age."[28]

In one of his essays, Montaigne has a personified Nature make this speech to man: "Imagine honestly how unbearable and painful to man would be an everlasting life. If you did not have death you would curse me incessantly for having deprived you of it."[29] The process of Nature is one of death and renewal. Who can doubt that if there were no death, if we were all immortal, life would become unbearably monotonous, and the feeling of "been there, done that," would eventually remove all the joy of living. If we lived forever on this earth, how would we spend our time? We might try different careers, travel the world repeatedly, and other diversions. Such things might help alleviate boredom up to a point, but in the end we'd be defeated by the one thing which we cannot prevent from becoming stale—ourselves. We try to pour new wine into old vessels, but over the years our "vessels"—the contours of our personality—become settled and fixed. The new wine begins to taste like the old. Over endless time, we would all become mortally jaded.

The French philosopher, Rousseau, one of Montaigne's admirers, makes a similar point in *Emile*: "If we were immortal, we would be most unhappy beings. It is hard to die doubtless; but it is sweet to know that one will not live forever, and that a better life will end the pains of this one. If we were to be offered immortality on the earth, who would accept this dreary gift? What resources, what hope, what consolation would remain to us against the rigors of fate and the injustices of man? The inevitability of dying is for the wise man only a reason for bearing the pains of life. If one were not certain of losing life, sometime, it would cost too much to preserve."[30] After all, if the goal of philosophy is growth in self-knowledge, as it is for most of the thinkers we've included here, then at some point living forever would simply mean the endless repetition of life's events. Most of life's lessons can be learned from just a handful of experiences so that the eternal repetition of such experiences would add little to self-knowledge.

Rousseau feels, then, that even if it were possible to extend our earthly lives indefinitely, in time we would all choose death. Death wipes the slate clean, Every time a child is born the world itself is reborn and renewed as the new consciousness sees everything with fresh eyes.

Nature's way, Montaigne observes, is cyclical. Again, Nature speaks to us: "If you have taken note of the revolution of the four seasons, they embrace the infancy, the youth, the manhood, and the old age of the world. It has played its part. It knows no other trick than to begin again. It will always be just this."[31] Furthermore, if no one ever died, the earth would become too crowded. In fact, if there were no death, it is unlikely that humans would ever have come to exist since it is the struggle for survival which serves as the foundation for evolution. Even just the slowing of the death rate resulting from improved food production and medical care has brought humanity to a precarious condition through overcrowding and disturbance of Nature's balance. Nature tells us, according to Montaigne, "Make room for others, as others have for you. Who can complain of being included where all are included?"[32] With literally billions of humans having come and gone before us, we are in good company. And not only have billions preceded us, but so will billions more follow us.

As is sometimes said, we are all a "child" of the universe. Nature was kind enough to bring us into the world, and when it takes us out it will not be an unkind act, but part of a larger plan which is ultimately good. Montaigne says, "Go out of this world as you entered it. The same passage that you made from death to life, without feeling or fright, make it again from life to death. Your death is a part of the order of the universe; it is a part of the life of the world."[33]

Although it's true that in the medical field, science and technology have given us powerful new techniques for overcoming illness and disease and extending our lives, it seems likely that it will always be a matter of prolonging the inevitable. One mathematician has calculated statistically that even if science succeeded in eliminating all diseases and also stop the aging process, even then few people would live beyond two hundred years. Even without disease and aging we would all eventually succumb to death in a hundred different ways: by auto accident, fire, drowning, plane crash, train crash, homicide, accidental electrocution, being hit by lightning, falling to our death, and on and on. Death will always be with us.

Montaigne assures us that not only does nature aid us in overcoming our fear of death, but so does our reason. The title of Montaigne's essay, "That to philosophize is to learn how to die," is taken from Plato who taught that philosophy can teach us to meet death without fear. For Plato, who was pre-Christian, death represented the freeing of the soul from the bondage of the body. Like Christianity, there is every indication that Plato believed in an afterlife. Consequently, he believed that the life of the philosopher is the way of life which best prepares for death or "practices" death in that it seeks to disassociate oneself from attachment to the body. The pleasures of the body have little lasting value. Only the contemplative life is truly meaningful. Plato sought to demonstrate how the life and death of his great mentor, Socrates, exemplified this. Although *Ecclesiastes* in the Old Testament may say: "How dieth the wise man?—as the fool,"[34] Plato wanted to show how Socrates, the wisest of men, dies, and it is not as a fool. Socrates died calmly with dignity, and in the total absence of fear.

Socrates had been charged with impiety and undermining belief in the gods through his incessant philosophical questioning of nearly everyone he encountered. The charges were trumped up, however, and were politically motivated. At his trial, Socrates presented his own defense, and while it was customary for defendants to be obsequious and apologetic, Socrates took a very different approach, suggesting that rather than putting him to death the city should reward him for his services in keeping Athens honest. In the end, in prison, Socrates spent his last day conversing calmly with his friends about philosophical matters, and when the time came to drink the cup of hemlock, he did so with total calm.

In the *Apology*, Socrates states: "For let me tell you, gentlemen, that to be afraid of death is only another form of thinking that one is wise when one is not . . . No one knows with regard to death whether it is not really the greatest blessing that can happen to a man, but people dread it as though they were certain that it is the greatest evil, and this ignorance, which thinks that it knows what it does not, must surely be ignorance most culpable."[35] Thus for Socrates the pursuit of truth, and the humility which must accompany it, help to dispel the fear of death.

And still, it is strange for Socrates to connect an awareness of our own ignorance with overcoming the fear of death. A very large part of this fear, after all, is derived from a natural human fear of the unknown. What death brings is unknown and it doesn't seem correct to say that an awareness of our ignorance about death will make us braver in facing it.

Socrates also states his belief that there are only two possibilities for death: it is either the permanent extinction of consciousness, or the individual soul persists in some form in an afterlife. For Socrates, neither are frightening. If death is extinction, then, he declares, it's just like the periods of dreamless sleep we have every night, which should be seen as "a marvelous gain." There are few days in our lives, according to Socrates, which can count as happier or more blessed than these nights of dreamless sleep. He states: "Now if there is no consciousness but only a dreamless sleep, death must be a marvelous gain. I suppose that if anyone were told to pick out the night on which he slept so soundly as not even to dream, and then to compare it with all the other nights and days of his life, and then were told to say, after due consideration, how many better and happier days and nights than this he had spent in the course of his life—well I think the King of Persia himself, to say nothing of any private person, would find these days and nights easy to count in comparison with the rest. If death is like this, then I call if gain; because the whole of time, if you look at it this way, can be regarded as no more than a single night."[36]

This is a surprising and somewhat mysterious statement for Socrates to make. If read carefully, it actually implies that with the exception of a very few days of one's life, death, as non-existence, is to be preferred to life. In other words, for the most part, non-being is preferable to being! This is consistent also with Socrates' last words to his friend as he drank the hemlock: "Crito, we ought to offer a cock to Asclepius. See to it, and don't forget."[37] Asclepius was the god of healing. Socrates' implication is that life is an illness and death is its cure.

When Socrates says that a single night of dreamless sleep can be compared to the "whole of time," this is very much like the eternity occurring before our birth, a time for us, you might say, of dreamless sleep. Most people don't look back on the time preceding their birth with great regret or sense of loss. For most it is of no real consequence that there was a time—a very long time—when they were not alive.

Does Socrates really mean to say that it would be better to have never been born? Or that we're "better off dead?" The Greek poet Sophocles, a contemporary of Socrates, declared in *Oedipus at Colonus*: "Not to be born is past all prizing best; but when a man has seen the light this is next best by far, that with all speed he should go thither whence he has come."[38] Socrates, however, appears to allow for the possibility that the pleasures of life may at times exceed non-being in his caveat that there can be some days in a person's life, however few, which surpass the blessedness of non-being. In this case, the goal should perhaps be to discover how one should live to maximize the number of such days.

If, on the other hand, our individual souls live on in the afterlife, Socrates states that he would simply do what he had always done in his earthly life, carry on a dialogue with the other souls of the departed in hope of gaining wisdom. No doubt, of the two possibilities presented by Socrates, the persistence of the soul in an afterlife is preferable to most people over an eternal night of dreamless sleep. However, many have sought to make the point that even if death is the permanent extinction of consciousness, it is nevertheless not a bad thing. Certainly, it would be the end of all pain. I've heard it said by people who do not believe in an afterlife, that, after so many years of struggle and strife, the thought of death as eternal rest is very appealing. They had lived their life as well as they could, often in difficult circumstances; now it was time to let go. What Socrates said was true—for those in this state of dreamless sleep, all of eternity is as nothing. Remember that Shakespeare in his famous, "To be or not to be" soliloquy, ends by declaring: "To die: to sleep; No more; and by a sleep to say we end the heart-ache and the thousand natural shocks that flesh is hier to, 'tis a consummation devoutly to be wished. To die, to sleep: to sleep; perchance to dream: ay, there's the rub; For in that sleep of death what dreams may come."[39] It isn't death that Hamlet fears, but of living again, of beginning to dream again, with its potential for nightmares. Dreamless sleep is to be preferred.

Many have brought our attention to the close analogy between death and sleep.* We talk of fearing extinction and yet every night we slip off peacefully to at least a brief extinction. There is a state of deep, dreamless sleep when we seem to be no where at all. It might be responded that when we go to sleep at night we know we'll wake up in the morning, but of course we don't really know this to be true. If we compare waking up with being born and going to sleep with death, then it appears as if Nature is telling us that death is preferable. How good it feels at night to let go—to let go of all of our cares and woes, and in fact, to let go of ourselves, and slip into blissful oblivion. H.L. Mencken, for example, comments: "The sensation of falling asleep is to me the most delightful in the world. I relish it so much that I even look forward to death itself with a sneaking wonder and desire."[40] And Montaigne writes, "It is not without reason that we are taught to study our sleep for the resemblance it has to death. How easily we pass from waking to sleeping: How little sense of loss when we lose consciousness of the light and of ourselves!"[41] And, he might have added, how unpleasant and unwelcome it is to wake up in the morning and have to summon the energy and courage to plunge back into our daily cares. If we give any credence to this analogy, the message is clear—death is to be chosen over life. Life is clinging and hardship and struggle. Death is letting go of it all.

---

* The etymology of our word, "cemetery," can be traced back to the Greek, "*koimeteriion*," meaning a place of sleep.

Socrates' assertion that there are only two possibilities—extinction or transmigration of the soul, and that neither is to be feared—is quoted often. Still, I think that if we approach it from a slightly different angle, there is a more comforting way to put it. In his *Meditations*, Marcus Aurelius focuses on the question of the *meaningfulness* of life, rather than simply its extension. He writes: "If gods exist, you have nothing to fear in taking leave of mankind, for they will not let you come to harm. But if there are no gods, or if they have no concern with mortal affairs, what is life to me in a world devoid of gods or devoid of Providence?"[42] In other words, if life is meaningful, then it is because "the gods" make it that way and they will not let us come to harm. Death need not be feared. If there is no god and life is therefore meaningless, then what does it matter if we face extinction? Aurelius is presenting essentially the same two alternatives as Socrates, but with a different more consoling emphasis. Mencken, again, said that the main objection to life "is not that it is predominantly painful, but that it is lacking in sense."[43] I think this is true. For most people, almost any pain could be endured if they were convinced that it was all for a higher purpose. If life feels meaningless, however, then death seems doubly so. Our death would seem far less frightening if we believed it to be meaningful.

Another way to put this is to say that there appears to be a powerful instinct in human nature to see our lives as a kind of narrative; its *meaning* is in this narrative. For most, this narrative needs to give some sort of expression to important values such as truth or self-knowledge or love. But since it is a narrative, or story, it also has an aesthetic component to it, an element of beauty. Every story, of course, must have an ending. This occurs with death. If the story is prematurely terminated, however, before the narrative has been completed, we tend to see this as tragic. It may lose certain components of beauty—harmony, symmetry, proportion, elegance, playfulness, closure, etc. It's not so much the length of time that's important, but whether the story has played itself out fully. A short life, or "short story" can be beautiful if the narrative is complete. When a personal narrative has run its course in a meaningful way, then death can actually seem to be a natural and aesthetically necessary part of the story. And the longest life can be tragic or "ugly" if its story is incomplete or fails to incorporate essential values without which there is no beauty.

In this context, we can almost see death as a necessity. A narrative which never ends would almost certainly suffer an eventual irreversible change of fortune. The same statistics which say that our story must have an end to it through accidental death, also mean that if it did not have an end, we would all in time fall victim to an accidental injury, physically or mentally, of an irreparable nature. Injuries which didn't kill us would leave us permanently damaged. The longer our lives, the greater the chance of such irreversible misfortune. At some point it would mean that nearly every story would end badly, no narrative would have a happy ending. In a manner of speaking, this is what begins to occur with old age, as we all begin to fall prey to the wear and tear of aging. In this sense, the fact that there is a natural limit to life should be regarded not only as merciful, but as good in itself. Indeed, it should be regarded with gratitude. Or, to put it another way, any story that continued without end would lose closure, and thereby lose its beauty. Although we say that some lives end in an untimely way through premature death, if our lives never ended at all, they would all, in a sense, become untimely, and eventually, suffer a loss of beauty.

But let's return to Plato's belief that philosophy is practice or preparation for death. What does this really mean? For Plato, it seems to mean two things. First, that the philosopher, by living a life of the mind, devoted to truth and knowledge, detaches himself from the desires of the body, and thereby prepares himself for an afterlife in which we exist as pure mind or spirit. But Plato also taught that the goal of philosophy is to see the "whole," the "big picture." If we can begin to do this, we can get a clearer understanding of our own role in all of it, a sense of meaning regarding our own life and death.

In the *Republic*, Socrates asks Glaucon, "'Do you think that a mind habituated to thoughts of grandeur and the contemplation of all time and all existence can deem this life of man a thing of great concern?'—'Impossible, said he.'—'Hence such a man will not suppose death to be terrible?'—'Not at all.'"[44] Plato may give his own examples of what he means by "contemplation of all time and all existence," but let's turn instead to Marcus Aurelius who, in pondering the courts of emperors before him, writes: "Think, let us say, of the times of Vespasian; and what do you see? Men and women busy marrying, bringing up children, sickening, dying, fighting, feasting, chaffering, farming, flattering, bragging, envying, scheming, calling down curses, grumbling at fate, loving, hoarding, covering thrones and dignities. Of all that life, not a trace survives today. Or come forward to the days of Trajan; again it is the same; that life, too, has perished. Take a similar look at the records of other past ages and people; mark how one and all, after their short-lived strivings, passed away and were resolved into the elements . . . All things fade into the storied past, and in a little while are shrouded in oblivion."[45] And in Book Ten of the *Meditations*, "Let your mind constantly dwell on all Time and all Being, and thus learn that each separate thing is but a grain of sand in comparison with Being, and as a single screw's turn in comparison with Time."[46] Even the Earth, he tells us, is like a speck of dust when compared to the vastness of the universe.

In striving to see the "big picture" or to attain knowledge of the whole, we're able to step outside ourselves, to see our own personal story as just one minuscule part of the infinitely greater panorama of human history, originating in the shrouded mist of the past and extending endlessly into the future. In this vast story of humanity we are allowed to participate in only the tiniest fragment. We begin to see our own life as just one variation on an eternal form or template. We see that it is we ourselves who are marrying, bringing up children, making a living, sometimes noble, sometimes petty, laughing, crying, sometimes frustrated, resentful, and despairing, other times fulfilled and joyful, and all the rest, until we finally play our small part in the spectacle and reach the end of our story. It's easy to be reminded here of the famous quote from Shakespeare that, "All the world's a stage, and all the men and women merely players; They have their exits and their entrances."[47] In this context, we may even begin to regard the thought of stepping off the stage and closing the curtains as comforting.

If we're able to perceive our lives in this way, we can begin to see it in perspective, we gain a more expansive view, and grow less attached to what seem like many of the small or even petty features of life. We may become slightly more detached from life, but also less fearful of death. The insight we gain is not that life is less valuable, but that we should welcome the fact that we are part of a much greater and magnificent whole. We participate in the cosmic drama in our lives and in our deaths. This in itself is one of the great benefits of philosophy, that *understanding* is a form of *participation*. The better we can understand the world, the more we're able to feel a part of it.

These considerations might lead us to an even more astonishing train of thought. Most of us have wondered at one time or another, "Why are we who we are and not someone else?" Isn't it just chance that we were born into this particular body, this particular time and place, and not some other? In his *Pensees*, the French mathematician and philosopher, Blaise

Pascal, writes: "When I consider the short span of my life absorbed into the preceding and subsequent eternity . . . Swallowed up in the infinite immensity of space of which I know nothing and which knows nothing of me, I am surprised to find myself here rather than there, for there is no reason I should be here rather than there, why now rather than then. Who put me here? On whose orders and on whose decision have this place and this time been allotted to me?"[48]

And yet, as the distinct individual that we are, we become attached to all of the singular facts of our life and ascribe infinite importance to it, but if we had been born as someone else, isn't it strange to think that we'd likely feel exactly the same way, even though all of the particulars were different! Such thoughts are like philosophical exercises which lead us gradually away from clinging so desperately to the seemingly random body and circumstances we've been assigned. We generally think of grief as an emotion of loss over the death of another—a good friend or loved one. But the sadness we feel at our own impending death closely resembles grief as we prepare to say goodbye to the one person we've known better than any other—ourself. In the degree that we can see ourself in the abstract as just one more narrative or story, randomly fallen upon like the roulette ball in the spinning wheel, we loosen our attachment and alleviate our sense of loss and grief—for ourself.

In the essay, "Of vanity," Montaigne discusses various options or preferred ways in which we might meet death. Much of the fear, he suggests, is not so much of death itself but in not knowing in what *way* we will die. How will it happen? When will it happen? Will it be peaceful or painful? Such thoughts activate our imagination and the fear of the unknown. Montaigne ponders his preferences among various modes of death. In a slightly comical passage he tells us that he would rather fall from a cliff than be crushed by a falling building; he'd rather be stabbed than shot; and that drowning is preferable to burning to death. Of course, a non-violent is to be chosen over a violent death, and the very best that could be hoped for is "that which comes from enfeeblement and stupor." How wonderful it would be, he writes, if we could choose the time, place, and mode of our own death. For this privilege, he says, he "would willingly give several days of my life."[49]

Aside from dying in a state of "enfeeblement and stupor," Montaigne asks what form a pre-planned death might take? "Might we not make it even voluptuous, as did the "partners in death," Antony and Cleopatra? . . .

There have been some, such as a Petronius and a Tigilinus in Rome, who, pledged to kill themselves, put death as it were to sleep by the comfort of their preparations. They made it flow and glide past amid the laxity of their customary past-times, among wenches and gay companions: no talk of consolation, no mention of a will, no ambitious affection of constancy, no discourse about their future state, but amidst games, feasting, jests, common and ordinary conversation, music and amorous verse. Could we not imitate this resoluteness with more decent behavior? Since there are deaths good for fools, and deaths good for wise men, let us find some that are good for people in between."[50]

Mencken, again, who seems to have so many clever insights into our mortality, declared that, "the hardest thing about death is not that men die tragically, but that most of them die ridiculously." Although perhaps that in itself is tragic. He goes on to say that if we could all make our exits, "at great moments, swiftly, cleanly, decorously, and in fine attitude, then the experience would be something to face heroically and with beautiful words." But no, unfortunately we are much more likely to depart of "arteriosclerosis, of diabetes, of toximia, of a noisome perforation in the ileocaecal region, of carcinoma of the liver." It sometimes happens that even great men whom we admire are reduced to absurdity at the end, "by dying of cystitis or by choking on marshmallows or dill pickles."[51] Mencken advises us wisely that we must have a sense of humor, not only to get through life, but to get through death as well.

Of course, as we've already noted, Mencken's observation about death applies equally to life. We can put up with a great deal of pain and hardship in life, indeed, we might even begin to accept the idea of death itself more gracefully, if we feel it's all meaningful. What defeats us more quickly is when life appears absurd or simply endlessly "weird," and reduces our personal story or narrative to a farce. Again, probably the best solution is to cleave to our efforts to make our lives meaningful, and as for the absurd part of life, follow Mencken's advice and laugh it off.

Chapter 3

Our Legacy

Montaigne's declaration that he had little to cause him to cling to life brings up the issue of death's timeliness or untimeliness. Are some deaths more timely than others? For Cicero, it is foolish to speak of anyone's death as timely or untimely, since fortune is so fickle. Normally, of course, we would say that the passing of an elderly person is more timely than that of a younger person or a child who has never really had the opportunity to experience a full life. We generally regard the death of a child as premature and therefore tragic, though, in truth, in Cicero's view we can have no way of knowing whether an early death might have actually saved that child from a harsh fate.

We know that after the death of his beloved daughter, Tullia, Cicero went into isolation and devoted himself to writing, including an essay on consolation upon the death of a loved one. Sadly, this work has been lost, but a half-century later, Seneca wrote, "To Marcia on Consolation, which compensates us a little for the loss of Cicero's work, and may cover much of the same ground. In his essay, Seneca attempts to console his friend, Marcia, on the death of her son. He assures her, soothingly, that those who die at a young age and seemingly have an untimely death, are actually more blessed. "It is true that the souls that are quickly released from interaction with men find their journey to the gods above most easy; for they carry less weight of earthly dross. Set free before they become hardened, before they are too deeply contaminated by the things of earth, they fly back more lightly to the source of their being, and more easily wash away all defilement and stain."[52]

Both Seneca and Cicero give examples from their own time, expressing their view that it may often be more timely to end our lives sooner rather than later. Drawing on Homer's *Iliad*, Cicero says that, as King of Troy, Priam had led an auspicious life of great prosperity, numerous sons, honor, and power, yet had the misfortune to live long enough to see it all taken from him when the Greeks sacked the city. He himself was put to death by Neoptolemus, the son of Achilles. Wouldn't it have been better, Cicero asks, if death had taken Priam earlier, with his sons alive and his throne secure?

Regarding the Roman civil wars between Caesar and Pompey, Cicero asks us, "Our dear friend Pompey, on the occasion of his serious illness at Naples, got better . . . Public congratulations poured in from the towns . . . Had his life come to an end then, would he have left a scene of good or a scene of evil? Certainly he would have escaped wretchedness. He would not have gone to war with Caesar, he would not have taken up arms unprepared, he would not have left home, he would not have fled Italy, would not have lost his army and fallen unprotected into the hands of armed slaves; his poor children, his wealth, would not have passed into the power of his conquerors. Had he died at Naples, he would have fallen at the zenith of his prosperity, whilst by the prolongation of life what repeated, bitter draughts of inconceivable disaster he came to drain!"[53] Thus according to Cicero, it is foolish to speak of death as either timely or untimely. Since it is impossible for us to know what the future holds, we may often fear something which is actually a blessing, and long for something which will actually lead to calamity.

Seneca, born about forty years after Cicero's death, decided, again, in his "To Marcia on Consolation," to add Cicero himself to the list of those who might have been better off to have ended their life earlier. "If Marcus Cicero had fallen at the moment when he escaped the daggers of Cataline . . . If he had fallen as the savior of the commonwealth which he had freed, if his death had followed close upon that of his daughter, even then he might have died happy. He would not have seen swords drawn to take the lives of Roman citizens, nor assassins parceling out the goods of their victims in order that these might even murdered at their own cost, nor the spoils of a consul put up at public auction, nor murders contracted for officially, nor brigandage and war and pillage."[54] As it happens, Cicero was put to death by Marc Antony, one of the three triumvirs ruling Rome after the assassination of Caesar. And if we were to carry this one step further, we could, in turn, add Seneca to the list of those who might have died a more timely death if it had taken place before he was ignobly executed by Nero.

Our deaths, perhaps, are more likely to be timely if we live our lives in a timely fashion. Montaigne felt that those who had lived long lives should prepare themselves to leave the stage. He himself was prepared to do so because he no longer had great family obligations or other unfinished business to detain him. In our advanced years, he suggested, we should not be formulating endless projects for ourselves. "The young man should make his preparations, the old man enjoy their fruits, say the sages. And the greatest defect they observe in our nature is that our desires incessantly renew their youth. We are always beginning to live over again. Our study and our desire should sometimes savor of old age. We have one foot in the grave, and our appetites and pursuits are just being born."[55]

In this respect, Montaigne's advice reminds one of the prescription of Eastern religion, particularly Hinduism, which recommends a different approach for the various stages or seasons of life. The first stage, that of youth and adolescence, is the time for learning, the developing of good habits, and the formation of character. The second stage is that of marriage and the cultivation of the duties and pleasures of family, vocation, and community involvement. The individual is at the zenith of their energy and can continue to learn in fulfilling the roles of householder, worker, citizen. The third stage, the autumn of life, is retirement. The individual can withdraw from many of their former obligations and now spend time pondering the meaning of it all. This is the philosophical stage of life. And finally, with the fourth stage of advanced age, has come the true time for detachment. The desires have waned. There is nothing that must be proved or accomplished. With regard to the lessons that life has to teach, the individual has "been there, done that." This is the true time for disengagement according to the natural seasons of life.

Montaigne asserts that as he as grown older he has learned to free himself of never-ending projects. "The longest of my plans has not a year in extent. Henceforth I think of nothing but making an end; I rid myself of all new hopes and enterprises; I take my last leave of every place I go away from, and dispossess myself every day of what I have."[56] Similarly, Cicero said of himself, "Indeed, if some god granted me the power to cancel my advanced years and return to boyhood, and wail once more in the cradle, I should firmly refuse. Now that my race is run, I have no desire to be called back from the finish to the starting point!"[57]

Still, there are those who disagree with Montaigne. It's true that setting aside the tail-end of our life as a time of quiet reflection is not a bad thing; we may be able to review our lives and better understand past successes and failures. But it is a little like putting the cart before the horse. If we had spent more time in reflection in our younger years, we might have made fewer mistakes in the first place. Philosophical reflection is something which should not be put off until old age. And, of course, Montaigne himself does not do so.

Some philosophers, including, apparently, Seneca and Cicero, believe that old age, rather than a time for retreat from life, is better employed as a time of vigorous activity, both in the form of recreation and actively contributing to society. Many people believe that our senior years, as a period when we're freed from many of the usual obligations of jobs and family, is the ideal time to give back to the community. If we feel we have gained some modicum of expertise or wisdom from our lives, this is something we can offer to the younger generation. Cicero, for example, in his essay, "Old Age," recites a list of famous figures from his own time who remained productive in their chosen fields—in public service, in military affairs, in the arts—far into advanced age. This is something we value in our own time. Fifty is the new forty, sixty the new fifty, and so on.

Joining Seneca and Cicero, Plutarch, the Greek philosopher and historian, also believed in the importance for those of advanced years to participate in the affairs of government. In his essay, "Whether an Old Man Should Engage in Public Affairs," he informs us that even though older citizens may lack their former physical strength and stamina, this is more than compensated for by "the advantage they possess in their caution and prudence and in the fact that they do not . . . dash headlong upon public affairs, dragging the mob along with them in confusion like the storm-tossed sea, but manage gently and moderately the matters which arise. And that is why countries when they are in difficulties or in fear yearn for the rule of the elder men."[58] Plutarch brings our attention to the fact that the word, "Senate," in Latin means "body of elders," thus doing honor to the wisdom which comes with age.

This, as we've seen, is not Montaigne's view, who takes a more detached approach to life. "Unsuited for doing good or doing evil, and since I seek only to pass by, I can do that, thank God, without much attention . . . I am content to enjoy the world without being all wrapped up in it, to live a merely excusable life, which will merely be no burden to myself or others."[59] My own feeling here is that ultimately whether we choose to spend our final years in public service or active recreation or quiet reflection is a personal matter, depending on the individual's abilities, proclivities, and overall health. Perhaps best of all is George Bernard Shaw's advice that, "If you're going to die, die doing what you love to do."[60] As for Montaigne, he states that he would like death to find him working in his "imperfect garden."

We generally regard longevity as good but if we live into such advanced age that we begin to witness not only the deaths of our spouse, our siblings and friends, and sometimes even of our own children, we may consider this as having lived too long. Many people would also say that living to an advanced age of great decrepitude is not desirable. We value life as long as we are able to take care of ourselves without becoming dependent on others, and can maintain some quality of life. The more we're able to control the circumstances of our senior years, and eventually of our passing, the better. Cicero writes: "Age will only be respected if it fights for itself, maintains its own rights, avoids dependence, and asserts control over its sphere as long as life lasts."[61] Cicero's statement is amazingly topical considering that he wrote roughly two-thousand years ago. Some things never change.

This is especially true with regard to our own deaths. For example, it has often been noted that as hospital patients we tend to lose autonomy and acquire a mentality of dependence. Sociologists have described the process of depersonalization that occurs when we enter a hospital. Aside from doing a lot of waiting which immediately tells us that the hospital has all the power and we have very little, we are required at the start to disrobe, which in itself signifies a certain vulnerability and loss of identity. Then, somewhat like the branding of cattle, a little plastic band is placed on our wrist, indicating that the hospital has now taken possession of us. Most of our personal items are surrendered to the care of the hospital, to be returned to us if and when we're lucky enough to leave. In addition, patients are generally not allowed to roam around the hospital unescorted. Very quickly, patients realize that they have little power and must learn the rules of the game to survive. This is an overall strategy used by many large bureaucratic institutions, whether we're speaking of the army or school systems, but hospitals are especially effective at creating a sense of dependence, since the patient's illness already puts them in a position of great vulnerability.

This dependence on an impersonal institution can undermine the dignity of our final days. Instead of feeling at peace, we're more likely to feel upset and even more apprehensive and fearful. It's far better, if possible, if we're able to spend our final hours at home in familiar surroundings with family and friends. In this respect, the hospice movement has been valuable in helping with the care of terminally ill patients who wish to die at home.

If the goal is to diminish our anxiety, we may want to do such things as create a "living will" defining the circumstances under which we'd wish to have our family take us off life-support. Beyond this, when we have the financial means, it may even be a good idea to consider prearranging our own funeral and burial. Approaching the end of life is a time when it is easy for feelings of helplessness to overwhelm us. It may not be in our power to live forever on this earth, but taking care of those things which are in our power will help us to face death with greater peace of mind. And if we're concerned about loved ones we're leaving behind, this will alleviate some of their burden.

And, on a lighter note, as long as we're making plans for our burial we might also want to consider, as some do, an epitaph for our tombstone. They say that death is nature's final judgment on us, but an epitaph can be seen as an opportunity to have the last word. Some psychics claim that the dead can communicate with them, yet anyone, if they wish to have the deceased speak to them, need only walk through a cemetery and read the epitaphs. Indeed, the libraries are full of multitudes of authors wishing to speak to us posthumously. While some of these authors write immense tomes to convey their philosophy of life to the world, it's often possible to say just as much in a brief, pithy, epitaph of a few words.

This idea of the epitaph is interesting to explore from both a philosophical and literary point of view. The first decision to be made is who will write it. Many epitaphs, after all, are not written by the deceased but by those left behind. If we leave it to others to write, however, this might open up the possibility for one which is less than flattering, such as this anonymous epitaph:

> Poorly lived
> And poorly died
> Poorly buried
> And no one cried.[62]

The best way to avoid this, no doubt, is to compose it yourself. In many respects, the writing of an epitaph is a literary act, or perhaps we should say, a micro-literary act, a kind of epilogue or postscript to your life's narrative. For example, once we've made the decision to write it ourself, we need to decide, like all authors, who our "audience" is. Is our audience our immediate family? Then something as simple as: "John Doe: Beloved Husband and Father" may do. Only your family will know for sure whether this is fiction or nonfiction. However, if we write our epitaph only for our family and descendents, and those who have known and loved us, our "audience" will be very limited, since the day will eventually come when both our children and grandchildren are gone, and there's no one alive on earth who knew us.

Much better to compose our epitaph for a broader audience, humanity-at-large—or at least, anyone who might wander into the cemetery where we're laid to rest. Here, at least in our imagination, we can render our final verdict on the world to all posterity in perpetuity, or until the time that our tombstone crumbles and the cemetery is built over with condominiums.

Our next decision, at this point, is to choose our genre. If we're of a philosophical bent, we may choose something like this epitaph by dramatist Robert Keats:

> Life is a jest and all things show it.
> I thought so once and now I know it.[63]

Will Rogers chose this insightful epitaph:

> If you live life right death
> is a joke
> as far as fear is concerned.[64]

One might choose humor as their genre, like this one from Winston Churchill:

> I am ready to meet my Maker. Whether my Maker
> is prepared for the great ordeal of meeting me is
> another matter.[65]

Or possibly something reverent and inspirational as the epitaph of Benjamin Franklin:

> The body of Benjamin Franklin, printer, lies here,
> food for worms, its contents worn out,
> and stript of its lettering and guilding,
> like the cover of an old book,
> Yet the work itself shall not be lost,
> for it will, as he believed,
> appear once more in a new and more beautiful edition,
> Corrected and amended by its Author.[66]

If we have any poetic ability, we might choose something thoughtful like this epitaph by Robert Louis Stevenson:

> Under the wide and starry sky
> Dig the grave and let me lie,
> Glad did I live and gladly die
> And I laid me down with a will.
> This be the verse you grave for me:
> Here he lies where he longed to be.
> Home is the sailor, home from the sea,
> And the hunter home from the hill.[67]

As it happens, more and more people these days are choosing cremation over burial. Sometimes their ashes are placed in an urn and saved by family or placed in special "gardens of remembrance." Other times their ashes are scattered to the winds or disbursed in some location meaningful to the deceased. The final result in this case is that, at least in terms of their remains, there is literally no trace of their ever having lived. There is no place of burial, no grave or gravestone. This clearly makes an epitaph impossible, but perhaps having our ashes scattered is commentary of a kind. Burn the body, scatter the ashes, and pretend the whole thing never happened.

In the end, no doubt, the best legacy we can leave behind is not our epitaph but any contribution we've made to the world of truth or goodness or beauty.

Cicero reminds us that although we speak of lives as long or short, in the context of eternity all lives are like the blinking of an eye. He recalls Aristotle's observation of an insect near the river Hypanis which lives only for a single day. "If one of these creatures should die at the eighth hour, it has died at an advanced age; that which died at sunset is decrepit, and all the more if it happens on Midsummer's Day. Contrast our longest lifetime with eternity: we shall be found almost in the same category of short-lived beings as these tiny creatures."[68] Human life is like a brief flash between two eternities—the eternity of time before birth and the eternity following death.

Our conception of timeliness appears to be determined by our expectations. Plutarch tells us in his "Letter to Apollonius," that if the average life span were twenty years, then anyone living near that age would be considered fortunate and to have had a timely death. On the other hand, says Plutarch, if the average life span were two hundred years, we would mourn the untimely death of someone passing away at the age of one hundred. Today we have statistical surveys showing the average life expectancy for people according to country. We're told that the life expectancy here in America, for example, has gradually risen over the years, so that what once might have been a timely death now becomes untimely. We're also informed that many countries have a longer life expectancy than our own. The average citizen of Israel or France lives three years longer, the Australian four years, and the Japanese nearly five years longer. This has the odd implication that what might be a timely death in one country would be untimely in another. I suppose it could also mean, for example, that a Japanese-American dying near the average U.S. life expectancy would be mourned less by his American friends and family than by his friends and family in Japan who would see his passing as more untimely.

At the time of death, we'll return to the same state of non-being as before our birth, a condition without pain or cares. This is essentially the Epicurean view regarding death. Along with the Stoic philosophers, Montaigne frequently quotes Epicurus and his Roman disciple, the poet-philosopher, Lucretius. This makes it difficult to pin down Montaigne's position since the Stoics and Epicureans had very different philosophies of life and death. In any event, the Epicureans taught that death is extinction, and therefore the end of all pain and suffering. Hence, it is foolish to fear it. In his epic poem, *On the Nature of Things*, Lucretius writes: "Yet never a man misses his life and self / When soul and body alike lie lulled in sleep. / But we shall sleep like this throughout all time, / and we'll not miss ourselves—not in the least."[69]

I suppose this might be a consoling thought, and yet, once we have lived, the thought of non-being takes on a different light. The two periods of non-being—before our birth and after our death—do not seem equal. With life comes projects and hopes and dreams that didn't exist before, and which most of us do not wish to see terminated. And beyond this, there appears to be a primal fear of non-being. "Being" seems to be something desired in itself, even in the absence of life-projects. Plutarch calls the longing for being the oldest and greatest of all forms of *eros*. So overall the Epicurean position may not be that comforting.

Lucretius informs us in his poem that he will present the harsh truths of his mentor, Epicurus, in beautiful poetry to make them more palatable, much like, he says, a doctor who puts honey around the rim of a cup of bitter medicine to get children to drink it. But the "medicine" of the Epicureans is bitter indeed. They belong essentially to the school of thought which holds that death is not to be feared because life itself is so miserable. In fact, he writes, our earthly lives are hellish: "And all these things men tell of down in hell, far under the earth, are right here in our lives."[70] According to Lucretius, the suffering of the tragic figures of Greek mythology who were condemned to eternal punishment in the underworld—Tantalus, Sisyphus, Tityos,—are all paralleled in the earthly lives of the rest of humanity. All in all, it's unlikely that many readers of *The Nature of Things* will find sufficient solace in the "honey" of his poetry. As it turns out, Lucretius himself eventually committed suicide.

People sometimes pose the question, if they knew they had only a limited time, say, six months, left to live, how would they spend their remaining days? It's useful though to raise this question at nearly every point in life, since life is ultimately short for all of us and no one can be certain how much time they have remaining. It's always very timely and pertinent, then, to consider which things in life are of the greatest value. An awareness of our own mortality should make philosophers of all of us.

The important thing, Montaigne says, is not how long we live, but how well we use the time we have. "If you have made your profit of life, you have had your fill of it; go your way satisfied. If you have not known how to make good use of it, if it was useless to you, what do you care that you have lost it, what do you still want it for? And if you have lived a day, you have seen everything. One day is equal to all days. There is no other light, no other night. This sun, this moon, these stars, the way they are arranged, all is the very same your ancestors enjoyed and that will entertain your grandchildren."[71] The more poorly we use our time in life, leaving the important things undone, the more untimely our death will seem.

Elsewhere in his *Essays*, Montaigne discusses the thought from Ovid that no judgment can be made as to the happiness of a person's life until it has ended. Ovid's lines are: "No man should be called happy til his death; Always we must await his final day,/Reserving judgment til he's laid away."[72] This can mean different things. It may mean that good fortune may shine on someone nearly all their life and yet turn against them at the end. Or it may mean that someone who has been strong and noble all their life may lose their nerve at the end. An otherwise courageous person may face death in fear and trembling. Montaigne writes: "In everything else there may be a sham: the fine reasonings of philosophy may be a mere pose in us; or else our trials, by not testing us to the quick, give us a chance to keep our face always composed. But in the last scene, between death and ourselves, there is no mere pretending . . . We must show what there is that is good and clean at the bottom of the pot."[72]

I can't help but think that in neither of these cases is it fair to judge the value of a person or their life. We've already examined the issue of the unpredictability of fortune. However, I believe all of these philosophers would agree that as long as one keeps their eye on the ball and devotes their life to those things most needful, they need not fear a "reversal of fortune," even in the form of death. The Stoics taught that we should learn to be above fortune, that is, that one's happiness should not depend on exterior circumstances. Aristotle, though not a Stoic, makes a similar point: "Fortune's wheel often turns upside down for the same person. For clearly, supposing that we follow the guidance of his fortunes, we shall often call the same man by turns happy and miserable, representing the happy man as a sort of 'chameleon," a cast in the sand. Probably it is not right at all to follow the change of a man's fortunes, because success and failure in life do not depend on these . . . It is virtuous activities that determine our happiness."[73]

I like what the Greek Stoic philosopher, Epictetus, (not to be confused with Epicurus), writes on the subject: "What is it then, you wish to be doing when death finds you? I, for my part, should wish it to be some work that befits a man, something beneficent, that promotes the common welfare, or is noble."[74] In other words, a life dedicated to the most important things. And if our courage should still fail us at the end, we can rest content that God will judge us not by how we had died, but how we had lived.

Epictetus's advice that death find us doing something beneficent and noble is good, but even better, when a way can be found to arrange that not only are our lives a benefit to the world, but so are our deaths. Those who have the resources may arrange in their wills to leave money to worthy charities. Others may decide to have some of their organs donated to those in need. Best of all in recent years is the extraordinary instance of an African-American man who worked all his life as a janitor for a large American university, and through a lifetime of frugality and self-sacrifice, was able to save one million dollars which he willed to the university upon his death. I have no doubt that his gift and his name will be remembered at the school far into the future. It's difficult to think of any better way to guarantee that our life has mattered.

Even if we're not rich, we might still consider leaving some small amount to our favorite charity. I suppose the principle here is to try to turn something we usually think of as bad into an occasion for good. This is also one of the best ways for those left behind to honor the deceased and make a contribution to a good cause in their name. If your mother has died of cancer, make a donation in her name to an institution doing research to cure cancer. Many people who have lost children from deadly diseases have chosen to make their children's death the occasion, not just of heartbreaking sorrow, but of vigorous fundraising efforts to overcome and prevent the disease for other children. This is a wonderful way to honor the memory of the child they've lost. Earlier we spoke of the natural human need to see our lives or our loved one's lives as having a meaningful narrative. When a young child's life ends at such a tender age, it may appear to us to lack a meaningful narrative. The child's story has hardly begun. We, in our own way, can make their short lives meaningful in the ways that we've mentioned, by dedicating ourselves to a good cause in their name.

And at the end of our own lives we can do something similar in our wills and last testaments. If we ourselves are dying of cancer or Parkinson's or some other malady, we might leave a donation to the appropriate charity doing research in these areas. Needless to say, this approach of working to turn negatives into positives is a good policy not just for death but in life as well.

Although I don't believe that the world is a bad or evil place, many people, because of our very limited human perspective, feel that it is. This outlook, strangely enough, can actually give rise to a very positive morality. The goal becomes to be better than the world. If the world is harsh, then we can become compassionate and caring. If it is randomly cruel, then we can become consistently kind. If the world is indifferent to suffering, then we can be engaged and sympathetic. As I've said, I do not wish to condemn the world that God has made, and I have faith that everything serves a higher good which may be concealed from us, but those who think differently may find that their fear of death is diminished somewhat in feeling that they've lived lives more righteous than the world they were born into. Nevertheless, this sort of morality is based somewhat upon resentment and even "revenge" on a world which does not seem worthy to us. There may be a better foundation for morality. We'll talk about this a little more in the next chapter.

Thus, we can add two more approaches to our list on overcoming the fear of death. First, we will meet our end with greater tranquility and peace of mind if we feel our having lived made the world a better place in some way. Second, we may be able to make even our passing the occasion for the occurrence of some positive good, as with the janitor above. The reader will notice how in discussing death, we are brought in a natural way to a consideration of the best sort of life. Having led the right kind of life allows us to meet death with fewer regrets, and even a sense of satisfaction and accomplishment, a "job well done."

Many Buddhists believe that a person's frame of mind when they're near death determines their path after death, for instance nirvana or rebirth. Though I don't literally believe this, we can sense intuitively that there is value in meeting death with a composed and tranquil mind rather than a heart full of rage and resentment. A part of possessing some sort of peace of mind at the end of life depends on how we look back and reflect on our life. If we've learned from our mistakes, we need not dwell endlessly on unpleasant memories or regrets. Instead, we should remember as much of the good as we can, good that we've done and good that has come our way during our lifetime. We may not have been saints, but nearly everyone has done some good. Remember your good deeds or kindnesses to others. If there have been too few of these, perhaps you've been a good friend or spouse or parent. They say that some people at the end, pat themselves on the back for never having killed anyone (God knows the temptation), or for never having gone to jail, and other such accomplishments. As silly as this sounds, I think it makes sense that, if we can't praise ourself for having done much good, then we might as well praise ourself for having done little harm. Certainly, Montaigne did so in his efforts to live "a merely excusable life." And, in fact, in the world such as it, where it is often profitable to do harm, it is a fairly notable achievement to not do so.

You might also, in your final days, recall the good that has come to you—small successes, good people you've known, happy times in general. By reflecting on our lives in this way we can make it possible to leave our earthly life behind with gratitude and a sense of satisfaction rather than regrets or bitterness.

Some say that when we die, we're asked by a guiding spirit to show them a review of our lives, particularly what we might have learned. This, of course, is a good practice not only when we're near death but all through life. Seneca said that each night at the end of a long day he reviewed the day's events for successes and failures, helping him to become a better person in the future. But when we review our lives at the end of a long life, we should do it in a forgiving way, forgiving to others, and forgiving to ourselves.

Chapter 4

Socrates' Second Alternative

Much of what has been said thus far allows for the possibility that there is no afterlife. It seems to me though that if this is the case, we can say that death or oblivion is good only if life itself is bad: Life is bad; therefore death is good. Certainly, if life is truly bad, we may as well welcome death rather than fear it. This appears to be Plato's message when he argues that philosophy is "preparation for death." Through philosophy we learn to diminish our attachment to life. For Plato, during our life on earth, our souls are "imprisoned" in our body, and death brings release from this prison.

It should be noted that Montaigne is not among those who say that death is good because life is bad. He states clearly: "As for the opinion that disdains our life, it is ridiculous. For after all, life is our being, it is our all. Things that have a nobler and richer being may accuse ours; but it is against nature that we despise ourselves and care nothing about ourselves. It is a malady peculiar to man, and not seen in other creatures, to hate and disdain himself."[75]

Is it really true that life is essentially bad? Much of it is, no doubt, but for most people there are also moments of love and laughter and even joy. If we were to try and decide if life were basically good or bad on the basis of whether on balance we experienced more pleasure or pain, we'd probably have to begin by saying that it all depends on the individual—for some people the pleasures outweigh the pain, for others the pains seem to outweigh the pleasures. Some are more fortunate, some less. Rousseau, however, suggested that even after we have subtracted all of the things we ordinarily think of as pains and pleasures, we are still left with the sheer sensation of existence, of being alive, which, he felt, was in itself a very pleasurable sensation. This is something like the experience of sitting on a park bench on a lovely day, soaking up the sights and sounds, and watching the world go by. Including this state of mind would tip the balance in favor of affirming life as essentially good, since most of us, most of the time, are neither in pain nor pleasure, but simply alive and open to the world around us, something like "witnesses" to life, and this is itself pleasurable.

Beyond the pleasure of the pure sentiment of existence, which can probably be described as an essentially receptive state of mind, we should add the fact that life can also be extraordinarily *interesting*. Most of us are able to experience a sense of wonder at the beauty and mystery of existence. We have the feeling that there is something greater than ourself, something from which we came, of which we're a part, but may not completely understand. To see the world as "interesting" may be a less intense form of wonder, but it is more *engaged*. For the active mind, the world is a curious and profoundly interesting place to live. Edmund Burke wrote that, "The first and simplest emotion which we discover in the human mind is curiosity."[76] Even the puzzle of how to overcome the suffering in the world can be the source of considerable fascination and intellectual challenge.

And the pleasure which comes from actually solving such puzzles and arriving at an *understanding* of the world shouldn't be underestimated. It's strange, I think, that our language doesn't seem to have a common term for the pleasure or emotion felt when we come to understand something for the first time. At times it can be an epiphany, as when Archimedes shouted, "Eureka!" upon his great mathematical discovery. In this case, it approximates exhilaration or exultation, a sense of triumph. It more everyday cases, it may express itself in a feeling of modest pride or self-satisfaction. It's sometimes said that while most of the animal kingdom seem truly "native" or to truly belong to the earth, humans, with an intelligence that seeks meaning and understanding, often feel like aliens or strangers in a strange land. The more we understand the world, however, the more we bring ourselves into harmony with it. Understanding brings us a sense of being more "at home" in the world, of knowing better our place in the scheme of things, or how we "fit." In other words, understanding is itself a pleasure, and, to that extent, a relief from feelings of alienation or estrangement.

Thus, all of these, the pleasure of the sheer sentiment of being alive, the "interestingness" of life, that is, the intellectual stimulation we experience when we puzzle over life's mysteries; and finally, the pure delight of understanding when we feel ourselves brought closer to the truth, all point to the goodness of life and the preponderance of pleasure over pain. God has given us mysteries to solve and the mental tools to seek a solution. What could be better? These pleasures are available to everyone at some level. Together, along with life's many other pleasures—love, beauty, laughter, joy—they tip the scales greatly in favor of the positive affirmation of life. Contrary to Plato, this may be the real sense in which philosophy prepares us for death, not by detaching us from our bodies or the physical and material worlds, but rather learning a *wise* attachment to the good things of this world.

We can go still beyond this and say that even those things in life which we usually think of a causing pain or suffering can serve a very positive purpose in making us stronger and wiser. This is how we grow as a person. The trials and tribulations of life cause us to turn inward in order to cope, and in the process we often find greater self-knowledge and fortitude. Seneca, for instance, says of the person who has never really been challenged by life, "I account you unfortunate because you have never been unfortunate. You have passed through life without an adversary; no one can know your potential, not even you. For self-knowledge, testing is necessary."[77]

When you think about it, if we sincerely believed that life is essentially bad, or even just more bad than good, then this would have the rather profound implication that it would be sinful to have children. After all, to make the decision to have children is equivalent to forcing someone to come into this world, who, of course, had not asked to be born. If we really believe this world to be too harsh or malevolent, this would be bordering on an act of evil, almost like the kidnapping or forced abduction of a soul. However, for the reasons already given, this is not likely to be the case and bringing a new soul into the world is, for that soul, the first step in a long process of ascension.

Let us conclude that life is essentially good, but not, therefore, that death is bad. There is another possibility: that life is inherently good and that those things in life which seem bad are actually training for an afterlife which is better still.

Many philosophers have extolled the satisfactions of intellectual pursuits over those of the body. The pleasures of the mind, of course, should take priority even for younger people, but they are particularly well-suited for those who are elder. Wisdom is supposed to be the special virtue of those of advanced years. Cicero says, "If a man is sensible and well-educated, his taste for intellectual pursuits increases with the years. So there is truth in Solon's observation that as he grew older he learnt much that was new every day. And surely the satisfactions of the mind are greater than all the rest!"[78] And elsewhere he states, "When its campaign of sex, ambition, rivalry, quarrelling and all the other passions are ended, the human spirit returns to live within itself—and is well off. There is supreme satisfaction to be derived from an old age which has knowledge and learning to feed upon."[79] So I think that the approach of overcoming the fear of death by arguing that death is good because life is bad is not the wisest overall.

Montaigne points out that it's not so much death itself that frightens us, it's the approach of death, the anticipated pain of it. But death, he says, is really the end of all pain. "Furthermore, this should console us, that in the course of nature, if the pain is violent, it is short; if it is long it is light. You will not feel it very long, if you find it too much; it will put an end to itself, or to you; both come to the same thing. If you cannot bear it, it will bear you off."[80] Montaigne also quotes Cicero: "Remember that death ends the greatest ills, that the small ones have many intervals of respite, and that we are masters of the moderate ones; so that if they are bearable we shall bear them; if not we can leave life as we leave a theater, when the play ceases to please us."[81]

As for the possibility of experiencing pain at the approach of death, for instance, from illness or accident, this is something that most people can learn to cope with. Many deaths, luckily, are not painful at all, and resemble falling asleep. And for those that are, we can learn to some extent to take in stride. Many people, from having experienced a measure of pain earlier in life, have already become adept at confronting it without any great fear. Pain is generally magnified by fear, but in experiencing and enduring it, it becomes much less frightful. Montaigne, in the midst of his painful bouts of stone, saw the opportunity to practice patience and endurance. "I test myself in the thickest pain, and have always found that I was capable of speaking, thinking, and answering as sanely as at any other time, only not as steadily."[82] In general, if we can live in a way that will toughen us somewhat, so that we won't be constantly trembling at the thought of the slightest pain, we'll contribute to our ability to eventually meet death itself with a calm demeanor. Thus, hardening ourselves to pain becomes one more method contributing to overcoming our fear of death.

At this point, we should take a minute to discuss a question which has been lurking in the background—the question of taking one's own life. Although I am strongly against such an action, some Stoics, such as Cicero and Seneca, argued that suicide is an acceptable option. When timeliness is the issue, doesn't death become perfectly timely when we ourselves choose the time of death? If the prospect of death fills us with feelings of vulnerability and powerlessness, doesn't our awareness of the capacity to take our own life put things back in our control? If we're frightened of the *way* in which we might die, then certainly, if we determine the time and place and mode of our own death, the way is no longer a concern. Will our death be sudden or shocking or painful? It doesn't need to be any of these things if we accept our freedom to make the final decision of life and death in this regard. This, at least, follows the general argument of Stoic philosophers like Seneca and Cicero on whom Montaigne so heavily depends.

Seneca, for example, declares that, "Living is not the good, but living well. The wise man therefore lives as long as he should, not as long as he can . . . Dying early or late is of no relevance, dying well or ill is. To die well is to escape the danger of living ill . . . The situation of humanity is good in that no one is wretched except by his own fault. If you like, live; if you don't like, you can go back where you came from."[83]

For the Stoic, the option of suicide is a matter of maintaining one's freedom. As they see it, without this freedom of choice we become a slave of circumstance. But the Stoics are not entirely consistent in this. We've already taken note of their belief that the hardships of life build character. Misfortune is merely an opportunity to become stronger and wiser. To be logically consistent, this would mean that we should never take our life on the occasion of any misfortune. We have a hand to play—we should play it out to the end and learn whatever there is to be learned, whether sweet or bitter.

In truth, in accepting suicide as an option the Stoics were out of step with the general tradition in philosophy. Even Socrates tells us in the *Phaedo*, "that we must not put an end to ourselves except under God's compulsion." The gods have given us life as a gift and it is not for us to throw it away. They are wiser than us and they know that even our suffering will serve some greater purpose. Socrates gives his approval to

42

what he calls the ancient doctrine, "that we men are put in a sort of guard post from which one must not release oneself or run away." This, he says, is a "high doctrine with difficult implications."[84]

In his essay, "A Custom of Cea," Montaigne discusses both sides of the issue. We commit no sin, he argues, if we decide to end our own life. "Just as I do not violate the laws against thieves when I carry away my own money and cut my own purse, or those against firebugs when I burn my own wood, so I am not bound by the laws against murderers for having taken my own life."[85] If suicide is not a sin, then there should be no punishment for it, in this life or the next. But Montaigne concedes that the reason for doing this must be extreme. He sees the virtue, when possible, in "sticking it out," and quotes Martial to this effect:

> 'Tis easy in bad times to look on death with scorn;
> Braver is he that proves that misery can be borne.'[86]

Fortune is inconsistent and even under the gravest circumstances we can have hope. Montaigne quotes the Latin poet Pentadius:

> 'The gladiator too has hope, prone on the sand, Although
> the thumb is down on every threatening hand.'[87]

Some Stoics may have believed that they could assure the timeliness of their death through their own volition, but when individuals make choices in a state of despondency, it is unlikely that their choices are completely rational. They have difficulty seeing that a better day may come. When people are in a state of great despair they become trapped in a very limited perspective. This is exactly the opposite of the goal of philosophy, which is to have the largest possible perspective on life, to see the whole. The only justification that Montaigne allows for suicide is unendurable pain, and even this, with the techniques of modern medicine, can often be made endurable. Montaigne has already said, remember, that if the pain is too extreme it is likely to end our life and mean the end of all pain.

I believe that many people at one time or another in their life think about the possibility of suicide and that this often occurs, most tragically, at a relatively young age, in the teens and early twenties, when all the unfairness of life is felt so intensely. As we get older we gain more perspective and the things that seemed so important in our youth no longer seem so. In other words, we become more philosophical.

If I were to offer my own advice, I'd say that we should never choose suicide. Life is already very short, and if we find ourselves miserable, nature has already provided a solution by making us all mortal. While we're hoping for a quick death, we sometimes forget that life is only the briefest flash. If life is a problem, it is a temporary problem. We have a certain amount of time allotted to us; Let's spend this time as we might spend money, as wisely as we're able.

Montaigne argues, as we've seen, that life should be seen as good in itself, or at least as much more good than bad. If life is essentially good, however, then it becomes difficult to argue that death is desirable. Unless, that is, the second half of Socrates' two possibilities is allowed for, namely the existence of an afterlife. And as it happens, Socrates himself, in the *Phaedo*, offers five reasons in favor of an afterlife. It isn't that Socrates believes these arguments are conclusive proof of an afterlife, just that they point in an intuitive way to the rationality of a faith in the hereafter. He indicates this at two places in the dialogue. After Socrates presents part of his argument in favor of a belief in an afterlife, one of his friends, Cebes, replies. "But I fancy that it requires no little faith and assurance to believe that the soul exists after death and retains some active force and intelligence." Socrates responds, "Quite true Cebes,"[88] and later in the dialogue after presenting a description of what heaven might be like, he adds, "Of course, no reasonable man ought to insist that the facts are exactly as I have described them. But that either this or something very like it is a true account of our souls and their future habitations—since we have clear evidence that the soul is immortal—this, I think is both a reasonable contention and a belief worth risking, for the risk is a noble one."[89]

It is interesting that Cicero, in his own way, echoes this sentiment: "Even if I am mistaken in my belief that the soul is immortal, I make the mistake gladly, for the belief makes me happy, and it is one which as long as I live I want to retain."[90] Faith, then, is noble. Of course, Plato and Cicero are not speaking of Christian faith, since both lived before the Christian era, but they are speaking of a certain basic faith that the universe is ultimately rational and benign. In contrast to modern philosophy which tries so hard to mimic the skeptical stance of science, traditional philosophy did not regard a belief in a benevolent God as prohibited. Even during the

Enlightenment we have Rousseau's advice that in the face of doubt we should always keep in our heart the *desire* or *wish* that the most important spiritual teachings are true, namely that there is a loving God, who cares about his creation. As long as we can do this, Rousseau writes, our heart is in the right place and we are blameless before God. Ultimately Rousseau teaches that rather than relying on reason alone, we should also consult our inner light. We should try to find the common ground between reason and intuition. The best path is that which is consistent with reason and against which our heart does not rebel. If we follow this path, even though we may never have perfect certainty, we are unlikely to go seriously wrong. It is only when we completely divorce our reason from our heart that we put our soul at risk.

Philosophy probably cannot prove the existence of an afterlife, but even in the absence of certainty, Plato states that such faith is a "noble risk." I'm reminded of these words by Tennyson from "The Ancient Sage:" "For nothing worth proving can be proven' Nor yet disproven: wherefore thou be wise, Cleave ever to the sunnier side of Doubt." For the philosopher (and scientist) it is not a question of faith in dogma, but faith in reason, faith that the universe is essentially rational, that it is governed by laws. And in some higher sense, to be rational is to be good. A rational universe seems to preclude a meaningless universe. It's true that this still allows for the possibility that the world may be good in some way that doesn't pertain to the welfare of humans, and yet, how strange if a rational world were not good for its most rational creatures!

Does Montaigne believe in an afterlife? Though at points he professes to be a Christian, he never seems to offer any justification, either religious or philosophical, for believing in an afterlife. If it were true that there is an afterlife, and perhaps a very blessed one, then this would be the greatest means of overcoming the fear of death. Indeed if there is an afterlife, then there is no death. But Montaigne speaks repeatedly of death as the end of everything. Nevertheless, Montaigne met his own end with relative calm and resignation when in 1592, at the age of sixty, he died from quinsy, an infection related to strept throat.

We would do better to turn to Montaigne's philosophical mentors, Cicero and Seneca, for an affirmation of the immortality of the soul. Just as Plato so often expressed his views in his dialogues through the persona of Socrates, Cicero chooses to use Cato the Elder as his spokesperson in his essay, "On Old Age." Cato reports that although he has spent most of his life working for earthly fame, "yet somehow my soul seemed to understand that its true life would only begin after death . . ." In the next life, he "looked forward to meeting the personages of whom I have heard, and read, and written. So when I start my journey towards them, it will be extremely difficult for anyone to pull me back . . . What a great day it will be when I set out to join that divine assemblage and concourse of souls, and depart from the confusion and corruption of this world! I shall be going to meet not only all those of whom I have spoken, but also my own son. No better, no more devoted man was ever born. He should have cremated my body; but I had to cremate his. Yet his soul has not gone from me, but looks back and fastens upon me its regard—and the destination to which that soul has departed is surely the place where it knew that I too must come."[91] Though Cicero has Cato the Elder speak with grief over the loss of his son, it's likely that Cicero himself had the recent death of his beloved daughter Tullia in mind.

But most beautifully, Cato (Cicero) advises us to "count nothing as an evil which is due to the appointment of the immortal gods or of nature, the mother of all things. For not to blind hazard or accident is our birth and our creation due, but assuredly there is a power to watch over mankind, and not one that would beget and maintain a race which, after exhausting the full burden of sorrows, should then fall into the everlasting evil of death: let us regard it rather as a haven and a place of refuge prepared for us."[92]

Seneca, for his part, writes: "The day which you dread as the end of your life is your birth into eternity . . . Dismiss with serenity limbs now useless and lay down that body you have so long occupied . . . Why stay attached to it as if it was part of you? It was only your hull . . . Eventually, the arcana of Nature will be uncovered to your sight, the mist will be dispersed, and bright light will radiate from all sides."[93] Elsewhere he tells us that in the next life our souls will be able to survey all of history, past and future. Here we will be able to "have the view of countless ages, the whole array of years; the rise and fall of future kingdoms, the downfall of great cities." In the afterlife, "no secrecy is here but minds are uncovered and hearts revealed and our lives are open and manifest to all, while every age and things to come are ranged before our sight."[94] These statements of Cicero and Seneca are remarkable when we realize that Cicero predated Christianity, and Seneca, although a contemporary of Jesus, knew nothing of the new religion.

Earlier we spoke of the importance of focusing on happy times in the past or on good things we've done as we approach the end of our life. Admittedly, the advice that we should displace fearful or disturbing thoughts with happy thoughts appears to follow the teaching of Epicurus. For life generally, I think this is not good advice since it prevents us from squarely facing and resolving our problems. In this case, though, our goal is to meet death without anger and regrets. And beyond this, if we are truly near the end of life, then perhaps it is time to let go of our endless struggle and contention with life's difficulties. At this point, there really are no further problems to solve other than meeting our end as peacefully as possible. In this one instance it may be worthwhile to follow Epicurus' approach. Along this line, one means of displacing negative and fearful thoughts is not just to meditate on happy memories and anticipations, but to consciously focus our attention on images which are pleasing to us which we find calming, particularly as it relates to the waning of life. Today we would call this form of meditation "visualization" or "guided imagery."

Cicero's image that in our old age we are like a ripe apple falling naturally from the tree is an apt metaphor and comforting in its way. If we follow Cicero's lead, another appealing image would be to picture ourself in the autumn, as a leaf changing color and preparing to detach from the tree. The weather is changing and the air is becoming crisp and cool. When the time is right, a soft breeze comes along, we let go of the branch and float gently to the ground, alongside the other leaves of the tree, and return to the earth, from whence we came.

Or we might choose another sort of meditation following Plato who teaches that we should seek to diminish our attachment to the body. We could imagine a kind of "etherealization" of our body. Picture yourself, for instance, standing in a meadow, on a small hillock, breathing in the clear, bracing air on a beautiful spring day. With each deep breath your body slowly fills with this pure, brisk air. As you continue, not only your lungs but your entire body fills with air, your chest and stomach, your arms and legs and finally your head. You feel yourself becoming lighter and lighter like the air itself. Eventually your skin itself becomes air, and as a cool spring breeze comes along, you merge with it.

A final suggestion which I find appealing is to ponder over the well-known poem by the English poet Thomas Gray titled, "Elegy, Written in a Country Churchyard," written at a time when many churchyards served as cemeteries for their parishioners.

> The Curfew tolls the knell of parting day,
> The lowing herd wind slowly o'er the lea,
> The plowman homeward plods his weary way,
> And leaves the world to darkness, and to me.
>
> Now fades the glimmering landscape on the sight,
> And all the air a solemn stillness holds,
> Save where the beetle wheels its droning flight,
> And drowsy tinklings lull the distant fold.
>
> Save that from yonder ivy-mantled tow'r,
> The moping owl doth to the moon complain,
> Of such as, wand'ring near her sacred bow'r,
> Molest her ancient, solitary reign.
>
> Beneath those rugged elms, that yew-trees shade,
> Where heaves the earth in many a mould'ring heap,
> Each in his narrow cell forever laid,
> The rude forefathers of the hamlet sleep.[95]

Grey's poem portrays death not as something fearful, but simply as a profoundly peaceful sleep. These are just a few suggestions for meditation. Each person will have their own choice of images which they find comforting. Reflecting on the peaceful images of a poem such as this or using other forms of meditative exercises like those above can help to calm our fears and assist us in letting go when the time comes.

At this point we can list all of those things we've discussed which can contribute to facing death without fear. Some of these are practical, some spiritual, but it's important to remember that philosophy can be both: practical because philosophy seeks to advise us on the activities of everyday life, and spiritual because it focuses on truth and love and beauty and how these may become an intrinsic part of our life.

1) Through mindfulness and mental rehearsal we can become more accepting of our own mortality and hereby less afraid. When

a loved one, such as a parent, goes through a protracted illness before passing away, we often grow slightly more accustomed to the idea of their passing from being led to reflect on it at length and imagine it in our mind. The same sort of thing might be applied to ourselves. We may find that by reflecting upon our own mortality, by mentally rehearsing it, the thought will gradually lose some of its sting. The Stoics taught that a large part of the suffering resulting from misfortune derives from its unexpectedness. The best antidote to this, they say, is foresight and mental rehearsal before the fact.

2) Try to see the big picture. Understanding brings distance and perspective. Your "narrative" or life-story is just one miniscule part of the much vaster story of humanity. If we can perceive our lives in this way, we can begin to see it in perspective, we gain a more expansive view, and grow less attached to what seem like many of the small or even petty features of life. As we become slightly more detached from life, we also become less fearful of death. As the distinct individual that we are, we are attached to all of the singular facts of our life and ascribe vast importance to them, but if we had been born as someone else, we'd likely feel exactly the same way, though all of the particulars were different! Such thoughts are like philosophical exercises which lead us gradually away from clinging desperately to the seemingly random body and circumstances we've been assigned.

3) In so far as possible, we should put our affairs in order so that unfinished business will not add to our distress. To the extent that we can do this, our death will be less "untimely."

4) Learn as much as you can to cope with pain. Most people, facing life's usual quota of challenges, find ample opportunity to do so. Physical and mental toughness will serve you well in life generally, and will also reduce your fear of death. Many Stoics, true to their beliefs, would deliberately put themselves in positions of great privation, for example leading lives of great austerity and even poverty although they possessed considerable wealth;

5) Be aware that you've not alone. Mortality is a part of the human condition and of all living creatures. Billions have passed before you and billions will follow you. And, we may as well add, thousands will die simultaneously with you. Montaigne writes: "Does not

everything move with your movement? Is there anything that does not grow old along with you? A thousand men, a thousand animals, and a thousand other creatures die at the very moment when you die."[96] You're in good company. When we look around us, we see that the earth itself grows old along with us and will some day come to an end.

6) If we have experienced the death of many others close to us, we may feel bereft and lost. Think of death as going home to loved ones who have already departed;

7) By living through the normal stages of life—career, marriage, raising a family, retirement—we come to a point where there is less to actively attach us to life. Our personal "narrative" leads us in a natural way toward disengagement. Allow yourself to begin to let go.

8) Nature, through the aging process, causes us over time to begin to accept our mortality with less trepidation. The illness and debilities of old age may gradually cause us to long for release. Let nature take its course and begin to let go.

9) Beyond the challenges of physically aging, the general struggle and hardships of life, the inevitable disappointments, failures and frustrations, often wear us down and disenchant us with living. Even for those who traverse life with no great tragedies, it still often happens that the endless middling annoyances and frustrations diminish our attachment to this world. Don't cling to this world but begin to let go.

10) At the lower end, we have the simple tedium and boredom of life. We may not be in physical pain or emotional turmoil, but simply lose our zest for living. We may have the feeling of "been there, done that." Our lives become redundant. If we were to live forever, this would inevitably become our dominant feeling. Such feelings don't mean that life is bad, but it is Nature's way of telling us that this phase of our education is over and that we should prepare to move on to something immeasurably greater.

11) If you can, live in a way to leave the world a better place. This doesn't have to mean a continual immersion in the lives of others (goodness). It could also mean the more solitary life of someone dedicated to the pursuit of truth or the creation of beauty in the world. This way, at the end, you'll be able to look back with a sense

of accomplishment and satisfaction, a job well done. Socrates said in the *Apology*, "Fix your mind on this one belief, which is certain: that nothing can harm a good man either in life or after death, and that his fortunes are not a matter of indifference to the gods."[97]

12) Explore the possibility of making your death the occasion for the occurrence of some positive good in the world such as donating your organs or providing something in your will for charity. Let your death itself become an occasion for an act of goodness. Knowledge of this will help to displace fear with something much more positive, a sense of self-pride in doing something noble and worthy for others.

13) At the end, reflect positively on your life. Think of the good that you've done. Even if you don't feel you've done enough, everyone has done some good in the world. Beyond good deeds, perhaps you've been a good friend, a good parent, a good spouse. And of course if you feel that you haven't done enough, it's never too late, as we said in the previous suggestion above. This will make it possible to look back with satisfaction rather than regrets.

14) At the end, focus on the good things that have happened to you in your life—good people you've met, happy times, small successes. This will make it possible to feel gratitude instead of bitterness.

15) Remember Marcus Aurelius's declaration that if there are gods, we have nothing to worry about since they will take good care of us, but if there are none or they are indifferent to our fate, then why should we regret departing such a world? Have faith in your heart that there is a blessed afterlife. A wise man once said that as long as it is your heart's wish that there be a loving deity governing the universe, you will be blameless before god. Such faith is a noble choice.

Since we began Part One with a humorous quote on death, we may as well close with another. Robin Williams said that "Death is nature's way of telling you that your table is ready." I like the way this is put. It's positive and hopeful. It's better, certainly, than death telling us that our reservation has been cancelled. Robin Williams' quote leads us to Part Two of the book, which argues that death not only tells us that our table is ready, but promises us a feast, a veritable banquet of truth and goodness and beauty.

PART TWO

A PHILOSOPHER'S VIEW OF HEAVEN

Chapter 5

In the Beginning

"I suppose that for one who is soon to leave this world there is no more suitable occupation than inquiring into our views about the future life, and trying to imagine what it is like."[98]

—Socrates in the *Phaedo*

Dante, when preparing to write his poetic vision of heaven, the *Paradiso*, admitted that he was "setting out on uncharted seas."[99] I know how he felt. Before we embark on our own perilous journey we might do well to say a few quick words about philosophy, which will serve as our guide or "rudder." Philosophers, when pondering life and striving to see the "whole," may have it occur to them that what they're looking at is not the whole at all. After all, if there is an afterlife, then our earthly life is only the "half." Indeed, if the hereafter should happen to represent an eternity, our earthly life is not even half, but only an infinitesimal part of the "big picture."

It may also occur to philosophers that if our earthly lives actually are the whole story, with nothing more beyond, it becomes immensely difficult to find meaning in it. Without an afterlife, our earthly life becomes something like Shakespeare's "tale told by an idiot, full of sound and fury, and signifying nothing." Or like Buddha's vision that, "All the worlds are like a flickering flame; they are like a shadow, an echo, a dream." Our life must "signify" something and yet it seems clear that this something is not self-contained in our life on earth. As we said earlier, death as extinction not only ends life but seems to devalue it as well.

In Part One of this book we tried to address the first half of Socrates' two alternatives, that death may merely be extinction. In Part Two we'll examine his other alternative—the persistence of the soul in an afterlife. It will not be our objective to try to prove anything with regard to the afterlife but simply to construct a kind of "working-hypothesis." What if there is an afterlife, then what would it need to be like to make our earthly lives meaningful? We'll try to determine as rationally as we're able what the content of such an afterlife would need to be. This is a question worthy of philosophy. Certainly, Socrates and Plato felt it to be so.

If we formulate our task this way, it allows us to examine philosophical concepts like justice, mercy, truth, goodness, and beauty in the light of our attempt to construct a sensible heaven. If we really had definite knowledge of the nature of the afterlife, we could then work backwards and determine the best sort of earthly life. How can we really run the best possible race if we don't know where the track ends? If the finish line is at the edge of precipice, past which we plunge into oblivion, it will be exceedingly difficult to make any sense of the race itself. In the above epigram, Socrates states that reflection on the afterlife and what it might be like is a suitable occupation for one who is "soon to leave this world." But surely, life is short, and in a sense we're all "soon to leave," so that speculation on this subject may be timely for all of us. Death should make philosophers of us all.

Philosophy can be thought of as a kind of happy medium between religion and science. Science is concerned with the "part," (atoms, cells, etc.) philosophy with the whole. Science seeks to know the "how" of things, philosophy the "why." The "why" is what we need in order to give meaning to our lives. Religion also seeks to know the why, but relies primarily on revelation rather than reason. Because philosophic endeavor is concerned with the why or purpose of things, it has a greater urgency about it than science. We might go about our lives fairly well without knowing for certain whether light is essentially a wave or a particle, but we'll have a much harder time if we have no concept of meaning or purpose for our lives. Even if we're unable to answer questions concerning life and the hereafter with certainty, each of us must still come to our own conclusions about the why and whither of life and death. There's no avoiding it. To not do so is simply to drift through life on the tide of received opinion, or to lead a merely random life. In the *Phaedo*, Socrates tells us: "It is our duty to do one of two things: either to ascertain the facts, whether by seeking instruction or by personal discovery; or, if this is impossible, to select the best and most dependable theory which human intelligence can supply, and use it as raft to ride the seas of life."[100]

This is essentially what philosophy is. It isn't usually possible to break down questions of life and death into tidy logical syllogisms, but it is possible to discern the broad choices and alternatives that life presents us with. Unfortunately, in choosing our personal philosophy of life we don't have the luxury, as do scientists, of testing it first in a laboratory. Our laboratory is our life. Probably the best criteria in determining if we've made the right choice is whether our philosophy is life-affirming and life-enhancing. Does it help us to thrive and flourish, and more importantly, does it engender such values as truth, goodness, beauty, love and joy in our life? Do we feel good about ourselves when we follow this path? This is the sort of criteria we must use in working out a philosophy to live by. If these things are true, then in time we may begin to regard our working-hypothesis as a full-fledged philosophy. The proof, as they say, is in the pudding. At this point, it may be regarded as a philosophy worthy of choice. We may choose to place our faith in it.

Images of the afterlife taken from our religious traditions have tended to be rather bland and unimaginative—one might almost say boring. Congregations of angels singing Allelieua for eternity and that sort of thing. It has sometimes been observed that our depiction of Hell, as portrayed in literature and painting is often much more vivid and interesting than our portrayal of Heaven. For instance, Dante's *Inferno* is more vivid and compelling than his *Paradiso*. The various religious traditions rarely have anything to say of a specific nature about "heaven" or the afterlife. Sheol, the abode of the deceased in Judaism, and the Greek Hades, were often depicted as places where listless, shadowy spirits passed their days. For the most part, they were joyless places. *Ecclesiastes*, for example, states that "There is no work or thought or knowledge or wisdom in Sheol."[101] And in the *Odyssey*, the ghost of Achilles tells Odysseus that he would rather live on earth as a lowly bondsman of an indigent farmer than to be king of the dead. In Hinduism and Buddhism, the afterlife appears to involve the complete loss of individual identity as the soul is absorbed and dissolved into the Brahman or Nirvana. Or it is reincarnated endlessly on earth with an indefinite postponement of the afterlife. And in the Gospel of Matthew, Jesus begins nine parables with the phrase, "The Kingdom of Heaven is like . . ." and yet somehow we never really learn what the kingdom of heaven is like, other than that it is very hard to get into. And even this assertion seems unreasonable to me.*

The Islamic *Koran* does present a fairly specific picture of heaven, though it seems mostly to express wish-fulfillment based on those things that are particularly lacking in many Islamic countries, such as water and shade. Still, to give credit where credit is due, I've collected every reference to heaven in the *Koran* and assembled them in Appendix A for those who are interested.

Any effort to construct a reasonable afterlife should be consistent with, and an extension of, our earthly life. It should be, so to speak, the other half of the puzzle—the two together forming a meaningful whole. For example, it should try to make sense out of the often painful and harsh nature of this life. Most visions of the afterlife—the beatific vision, staring into the face of God for eternity, even blissful concepts like the Buddhist *nirvana* or the Hindu *moksha*, etc.,—are basically non-sequiturs, and don't explain or justify the nature of our earthly lives. That's what we'll try to do here.

A friend of mine used to say that life is a test. The implication is presumably that we pass or fail the test and are rewarded or punished in some way in the afterlife. This tends to be the Christian and Islamic view of things. But I'm not comfortable with the idea of life as a test. It makes more sense to think of life as a kind of *training*. We don't pass or fail training, we may do better or worse, but the training never ends, in this life or the next.

There is an analogy told by Seneca which seems to throw light on the question of the afterlife, which goes like this: If a baby still inside the womb had a choice of whether or not to be born, it might choose not to. The womb feels comfortable and warm and safe, and the baby cannot even begin to imagine what sort of world is on the outside. The outside world is an unknown and seems frightening when compared to the security of the womb. The baby has no idea of the big, wonderful world waiting for it. In a similar way, the thought of death is frightening for us. Once again, we have no way of guessing what the afterlife might be like. It is an unknown. If we could, most of us would choose to stay in

---

* In John 14,2, Jesus does say: "In my Father's house are many mansions." Still, this is not very informative. It could be a description of the Hamptons.

this earthly life forever. And yet, the next world may be more wonderful and extraordinary than anything we can imagine here. You might say that in this analogy our body becomes a womb for the soul. Just as the baby spends nine months in the mother's womb in order to mature sufficiently to be able to survive and flourish in the outside world, so our bodies give us seventy-plus years to allow our souls to mature enough to be ready for the next world.[102]

They say that the first question of philosophy is: Why is there anything rather than nothing at all? Why does the universe exist in the first place? Wouldn't it be simpler if there were nothing? Scientists adhere to the rule that the best explanations are often the most simple or parsimonious. The explanations with the least variables are the most economical and elegant. What could be more parsimonious and economical than non-existence? What greater equilibrium could there be than nothingness?

And yet we find ourselves surrounded by a profusion of being. Modern physics tells us that there is a prodigious amount of power or energy in even the smallest amount of matter. If we consider the amount of energy in a star or a quasar or a galaxy of billions of stars, it is stupendous. All of this power expended for what? A wise man once said that to justify all of this godlike expenditure of power, there must surely be some truly wonderful purpose behind it all. Otherwise, it simply wouldn't be worth the effort. If there weren't an exceptionally marvelous reason behind existence, why go to all the trouble? It would be much easier to just "chuck it in" and lapse back into nonexistence. A meaningless universe would find a way to commit "suicide."

Such considerations seem to me like clues that the central principle of creation is a kind of *overflowing* or expression of superabundance. Creation is an overflowing. Love is an overflowing. Joy is an overflowing. Beauty and grace are an overflowing.

Skeptical philosophers and "realists" sometimes dismiss the idea of an afterlife as an outlandish fantasy. The real world is what they see around them, a mundane, solid world, generally devoid of the marvelous or miraculous. But I think that we come to this hum-drum view of the world around us through a gradual process that deadens us to the improbable novelty of it all. As a child, the first time I saw a live giraffe or elephant in a zoo, I wasn't especially impressed since I'd already seen scores of pictures of these animals. If I had simply stumbled upon such animals, never having seen an image of them, I would probably have been completely startled and delighted. It's the same, really, for all the world around us. From everyday familiarity we grow accustomed to it and lose our ability to perceive its oddness. But the closer we look at it, the more we realize how uncanny it all is. Perhaps Shakespeare's Hamlet had something like this in mind when he declared that, "There are more things in heaven and earth, Horatio, than are dreamt of in your philosophy."[103]

Montaigne makes essentially the same point in his essay, "It is folly to measure the true and false by our own capacity." He writes: "If we call prodigies or miracles whatever our reason cannot reach, how many of these appear continually to our eyes! Let us consider through what clouds and how gropingly we are led to the knowledge of most of the things that are right in our hands; assuredly we shall find that it is rather familiarity than knowledge that takes away their strangeness, and that if these things were presented to us for the first time, we should find them as incredible as any others, or more so."[104]

As we've said, the fact that anything exists at all is the first marvel. And beyond this, it isn't as if the universe were simply an infinite ocean of oatmeal, a formless blob. On the contrary, it has an intricate, complex structure. This is the second marvel. All it takes to see this wondrous nature of the world is a kind of openness or humility. Plato said that philosophy begins in wonder. An awareness of the mystery of existence sends us on a quest to understand it better. This wonder, in turn, leads us to humility. As Socrates taught, if he was wise at all, it was because he was aware of his own ignorance. The wise person doesn't presume to be in perfect possession of the truth. Again, this humility consists of an openness to the world. Our wonder brings us to see the world as "wondrous" or wonderful. The writer-philosopher, G.K. Chesterton, observed that, "The world will never starve for want of wonders, but only for want of wonder."[105]

Chesterton goes on to say: "The truth is, that all genuine appreciation rests on a certain mystery of humility . . . The man who said, 'Blessed is he that expecteth nothing, for he shall not be disappointed,' put the eulogy falsely. The truth is, 'Blessed is he that expecteth nothing, for he shall be gloriously surprised.' The man who expects nothing sees redder roses than common men see, and greener grass, and a more startling sun . . . Until we realize that things might not be, we cannot realize that things are. Until we see the background of darkness we cannot admire the light as a single and created thing. As soon as we have seen that darkness, all light is lightning, sudden, blinding, and divine. Until we picture nonentity we underrate the victory of God."[106]

Once we have realized how improbable the "real" world is, we shouldn't balk at the idea of heaven. Heaven couldn't be any more improbable than the world we presently inhabit. If everything we see around us is possible, then anything is possible, even the infinitely marvelous. In Part One, we compared death to sleep, and awakening to birth or coming into being. If the idea of death as going to sleep and never waking up seems odd, how much more astonishing is the notion of waking up without ever having gone to sleep! This is essentially what occurs when we're born. Pascal writes in *Pensees*, "What reason have they for saying that one cannot rise from the dead? Which is more difficult: to be born or to rise from the dead? That what has never been should be, or that what has once been still is?"[107] In effect, for Pascal, being born is the equivalent of rising from the dead. In other words, in being born we've all once "risen from the dead." If this is possible, why should we continue to be astounded at the concept of immortality, which is the persistence of that life? Montaigne, again, tells us that, "After you have established, according to your fine understanding, the limits of truth and falsehood, and it turns out that you must necessarily believe things even stranger than those you deny, you are obliged from then on to abandon these limits."[108]

It seems clear that there is a need in human nature for the marvelous, for something greater than the seemingly spiritless world around us. I'm reminded of the idea that Nature wouldn't give to its creatures needs which have no way of being naturally gratified. Nature implants in us needs for food, shelter, procreation, and the like, and it grants the means to meet these needs. But humans are also bestowed with a need or yearning for something "higher"—higher, at least, than what we find in our earthly lives. Why would Nature instill in us needs which have no way of being fulfilled? It would be "unnatural" to do so. Rousseau writes in *Emile*, that, "God, they say, owes nothing to his creatures. I believe that he owes them everything he promised them by giving them life. To give them the idea of a good and to make them feel the need of it is to promise it to them."[109]

It may sound unphilosophical to say that existence is "miraculous," but it's hard to avoid. Being, in itself, is miraculous. Miraculous because when we reflect deeply about it, existence seems vastly improbable. This is the first question of philosophy because it is the first challenge to reason, to explain something so startling. The second miracle is that existence is endowed with a beautiful and intricate design. And the third miracle, perhaps almost as astonishing as the first, that Nature has evolved to produce intelligent life that can look out at it with wonder and ask "why?" As others have observed, this is Nature becoming self-aware. But *why* should Nature create beings who can ask "why?" With the appearance of this question, all the concerns of truth and goodness, beauty and love, arise. And also questions of providence and the hereafter.

It's important to remember that it is Nature which has produced us and therefore Nature which produced the questions we ask. It is Nature which has produced beings which look out at the universe and insist on meaning. This insistence is Nature's insistence. It is Nature which has produced beings who long for a higher truth, a higher goodness, and a higher beauty. It has been said that this longing for something higher, for a more perfect world, is actually a longing for God. These aspirations may themselves be regarded as expressions of piety.

The great German philosopher, Immanuel Kant, regarded the presence of a rational moral imperative in humans as the best proof for the existence of a moral and caring God. He makes this point repeatedly in *Religion Within the Limits of Reason Alone*: "Yet there is one thing in our soul which we cannot cease from regarding with the highest wonder, and for which admiration is not only legitimate but even exalting and this is the original moral disposition itself within us . . . The very incomprehensibility of this predisposition which announces a divine origin, acts perforce upon the spirit and strengthens it for whatever sacrifice a man's respect for his duty may demand of him."[110]

For Kant, the presence of the moral sense in humans is evidence of both a just God and the immortality of the soul. In simple terms, Kant's argument is that man cannot be expected to live a just life in the larger context of an unjust universe. In an unjust universe the moral law would be invalidated and meaningless. The recognition of our own moral nature presupposes the conditions for its fulfillment—God and an afterlife. As one commentator on Kant has written, in our ethical behavior we need to be assured that "we are not acting in a world which nullifies our efforts, but that morality expresses a fundamental aspect of reality, so that in our doings and strivings it may be said that we have the universe somehow behind us."[111]

The perfection of the moral law in the human soul, however, is rarely possible in the span of a single lifetime. In Kant's own words, "For a rational but finite being, the only thing possible is an endless progress from the lower to the higher degrees of moral perfection." This perfection, "is only possible on the supposition of the immortality of the soul."[112] We are reminded again of Rousseau's statement that if God created beings who long for a more perfect world, or "heaven," then it can be said that he owes it to them. To create the need with no means of fulfillment would be unjust.

Although our focus here is on the afterlife and not on the existence of God, the two are inextricably linked. Without a caring God, there can be no heaven. Skeptical thinkers like the British philosopher, David Hume, contend that since questions concerning providence or an afterlife are beyond our ability to answer in any ultimate or final way, we should avoid them. In particular, following Isaac Newton, he argues that when we attempt to reason backwards from effect to cause, we must not go beyond the absolute minimum necessary to explain the effect. In the *Principia*, Newton states: "We are to admit no more causes of natural things than such as are both true and sufficient to explain their appearances."[113] For instance, in looking at the universe, it may be that it simply always existed and has no need of a creator, or if there is a creator, he may be indifferent to his creation. And, as Hume is quick to point out, if either of these is the case, we can dismiss any notion of an afterlife. In any event, in his essay, "Of a Providence and of a Future State," Hume writes that such questions exceed the scope of human intelligence and should be left alone.

Hume's rule of seeking the "absolute minimum necessary" cause to explain an effect begs the question. To posit a minimally necessary cause consisting of an indifferent god or a universe that always existed without beginning requires that the "effect" or the "given" be depreciated in value and reduced to dead matter. This is the "materialism" of science. But we've already argued that the "effect," the universe as we know it, is bordering on the miraculous and hence, of incalculable value. The cause, therefore, must also be upgraded accordingly.

I've heard the simple but powerful argument that if we had visited the Earth two billion years ago, we'd find a fiery, volcanic world, utterly devoid of life—a dead planet. If we returned to see it again in the present, of course, we'd find it teeming with an almost infinite variety of life. From whence all the life? From dead matter? Or is it possible, and even probable, that there is a kind of life-principle inherent in everything? Kant has his answer ready. In the *Critique of Judgment*, he states: "Absolutely no human reason can hope to understand the production of even a blade of grass by mere mechanical causes."[114] "That crude matter should have originally formed itself according to mechanical laws, that life should have sprung from the nature of what is lifeless, that matter should have been able to dispose itself into the form of a self-maintaining purposiveness is contradictory to reason."[115] Newton, it should be remembered, said that while the causes should not be multiplied unnecessarily, they must be "sufficient" to explain the effect, that is, not too few. For Kant, this must include a deity.

Likewise, the idea that the universe needs no creation and simply always existed seems lacking even by Hume's standards. In this case we have an "effect,"—the existence of the universe—without a cause. It simply "is." But this doesn't qualify as a minimally necessary cause or any other kind of cause. The universe becomes a causeless effect. Whether this sort of explanation really constitutes an advance in understanding seems doubtful. It might address the "how," but not the "why."

Another German philosopher, Gottfried Wilhelm von Leibniz, believed that it is necessary to explain not just that the universe exists but why this particular universe exists. We need what he called, "a principle of sufficient reason." This is the principle that "no fact can be real or existent, no statement true, unless there be a sufficient reason why it is so and not otherwise."[116] In adding this qualification, Leibniz makes the transition from the "how" to the "why." Why this particular universe? You might say that while Newton emphasizes that explanatory reasons not be more than necessary, Leibniz stresses that they not be too few. For example, to explain that there are elephants and giraffes because they have always existed might explain how long they have existed, but not why there should be elephants and giraffes.

In *On the Ultimate Origination of Things*, Leibniz writes: "Neither in any one single thing, nor in the whole aggregate and series of things, can there be found the sufficient reason of existence. Let us suppose the book of the elements of geometry to have been eternal, one copy always having been written down from an earlier one; it is evident that, even though a reason can be given for the present book out of a past one, nevertheless out of any number of books taken in order going backwards we shall never come upon a full reason; though we might well always wonder why there should have been such books—why there were books at all, and why they were written in this manner. What is true of the books is true also of the different states of the world . . . However far you go back to earlier states, you will never find in those states a full reason why there should be any world rather than none, and why it should be such as it is. Indeed, even if you suppose the world eternal, as you will be supposing nothing but a succession of states and will not in any of them find a sufficient reason."[117] And with respect to Leibniz's question of why this given world and not some other, we might refer back to our earlier question as to why there should be a universe which produces beings who insist on meaning?

Leibniz's principle of "sufficient reason" means that simplicity cannot be the only criterion. It must be simple but sufficient to explain the effect. The simplest explanation, after all, is solipcism—the belief that only I exist and everything else is a figment of my mind. What could be simpler? Or to use another example, the science of the eighteenth century is simpler than the science of the twenty-first century, yet it is not more true. Considerations of scope and depth must be taken into account.

The design of the universe is distinguished not only by its intricate order and harmony, but also by its beauty. Beauty in itself can be seen as a kind of superfluity. There is nothing in the existence of an orderly world which necessitates beauty. It's true that we often associate beauty with design, but the design of the universe could easily have been functional without being beautiful. Many human creations, such as a coal factory, embody elaborate design but are devoid of beauty. And yet, the natural world is saturated with beauty. This apparently gratuitous beauty speaks to us of something higher. When we experience the beauty of nature we sometimes have a sense of immanence or "presence" behind it all. There is a sense of rapport with something transcendent. We have a glimpse that perfection is possible. The quality of superfluity seems to express a condition of great abundance or overflowing. When we experience great beauty in the world we feel graced to witness a sort of miniature or microcosmic paradise. We are blessed with the insight that if beauty is possible here, even in this imperfect world, it must be possible on a grander scale, a universal scale.

In this sense, it has been said, beauty is a promise, or perhaps a "mini-salvation," promising a fuller salvation. We see that beauty is not only conceivable, it is actual, it exists, if only in microcosm. This glimpse or promise of perfection may send us on a quest, not just an aesthetic quest, but an intellectual and spiritual quest for the truth behind the beauty—a quest for the content of this perfect world, glimpsed in beauty. In this regard, beauty could be seen as a *summons*.

Indeed, great beauty often seems like more than a promise. In the moment that we're caught up and absorbed in it, we have a sensation of certitude; we have pierced the veil and seen the radiance on the other side. There is a distinct sensation that the source of this radiance could only be a divine beatitude shining through. If the universe and the natural world were uniformly ugly or predominantly so, it's far less likely that anyone would be inspired with thoughts of god or a more perfect world.

Even if we were to speak simply of probabilities rather than certainties, we're justified in asking whether it is more probable that the intricate and beautiful design of nature has reason and purpose behind it, or that it is random and pointless? The case could be made that the "minimally necessary," in terms of cause and effect and the "how" of things, is also the *minimally probable* in terms of means and ends and the ultimate "why" of things. Our goal should be to seek the most probable explanation.

Richard Swinburne, in his book *The Existence of God*, argues that although the various theories for the existence of god are not conclusive individually, each makes such existence more probable, and all the more so when added together. The probability of the existence of god is cumulative and grows with the addition of each of these considerations. Collectively they make the existence of God highly probable. Or to put it another way, in the *absence* of god, each of these conditions—the existence of anything at all, the existence of a universe of intricate order, the evolution of creatures who long for meaning, and the remarkable, seemingly gratuitous beauty of the world—all become exceedingly *improbable*. They only become probable as the product of divine providence. As Cicero writes in the preface to *The Nature of the Gods*, "We can attain only to a number of probable truths, which although they cannot be proved as certainties, yet may appear as clear and convincing that a wise man may well adopt them as a rule of life."[118]

In this chapter, I've tried to simplify and conflate the various arguments supporting the existence of God. Down through the centuries such arguments have acquired impressive names, like the ontological argument, the cosmological argument, the teleological argument, etc. Swinburne believes, for example, that if we take the existence of God as being a 50-50 proposition, then the fact that something exists rather than nothing might be thought to make it 60-40 in support of God. If we add to this the fact that existence has an intricate design, the probability in support of God may improve to something like 70-30. The evolution of conscious beings who aspire to a higher truth, goodness, and beauty could be said to yield an 80-20 probability; and finally, the beauty of Nature might improve the odds to something like 90-10 in support of God's existence. Swinburne does not use these numbers; I give them only as an example of his general meaning.

Hume's contention that, if there is a creator, he may be indifferent to his creation, doesn't seem credible to me. It's clear that Hume has some respect for the view that an intricately structured universe may imply an intelligent creator or "designer," but even when he allows for this possibility, he rejects the notion that this creator would be a caring or loving god, since he sees around him a world which is so often harsh and cruel in its effects on humankind. Aside from the argument presented in Part One that human life is far more good than bad, and that some measure of suffering is training for the soul, I would add that a rational god also implies a caring god. It is our reason which gives us the ability to discriminate between right and wrong and become moral beings. It seems that God, as the most rational of all beings, would also be the most moral. My own feeling is that once we allow for the possibility of an intelligent creator, we can't help but make the observation that it is natural for all "creators" to love their creations. Artists love their paintings, composers love their compositions, authors love their books, mothers love their children, and yes, Gods or "Creators" must love their creations.

The editor of a recent collection of Hume's writings on religion admits that Hume's skeptical premises are severely restricting. "At one blow," he says, "they invalidate practically every interesting conclusion which anyone could wish to draw."[119] In other words, skeptical philosophy, like science, prevents us from asking "why" regarding the ultimate questions. It might be argued that this is not philosophy at all, but the abandonment of philosophy in favor of science. Although the scientific project of determining the "how" of everything may be exceedingly valuable, in itself it isn't enough. We must be allowed to ask *why* for the reasons already given. We could even assert that we have a moral obligation to do so.

Chapter 6

Perfect Justice

Breakthroughs in philosophy and science often come when two seemingly incompatible or contradictory explanations are resolved. For example, in physics, experiments show that light sometimes behaves as a particle and other times as a wave. Yet it seems illogical that it could be both. When the apparent contradiction is finally resolved it will no doubt lead to a deeper understanding by physicists of the phenomenon involved. The same sort of approach can apply in philosophy. For instance, humans have two moral ideals which they hold in high esteem but which are in conflict with each other. One is *justice*, which Plato defined as "to each his due." The bad deserve to be punished and the good rewarded. All of us are outraged and indignant when we learn of bad people going without punishment, and perhaps also when good people go without reward. We try to incorporate these principles in our social institutions—the jails take care of the bad, and the good are rewarded in various ways through community recognition, esteem, and so forth.

The other moral ideal is mercy or forgiveness. Unlike justice, mercy is not giving to each his due, but giving to each perhaps more than their due. We should have mercy on the wrongdoer, even if, strictly speaking, they don't seem to deserve it, since it is possible that there are circumstances beyond their control or that they simply "know not what they do." We should seek to forgive them and even have compassion for them. This is a noble ideal and comes to us particularly through our Christian heritage. We also try to incorporate mercy into our justice system as a way of softening the harsh demands of strict justice. Courts try to recognize "extenuating circumstances" that might lessen the punishment.

Hence both justice and mercy are worthy ideals which we all hold high, but, by definition, as we've seen, they are incompatible. One is giving to each his due, the other is giving to each more than their due.

What is especially interesting here, though, is when we try to ascribe these ideals to our concept of a deity. We wish to see God as the administrator of perfect justice. If we are unable in this world to adequately punish all the wrongdoers and reward all the righteous, then God will do so in the next world. We long for the evildoers to "get their due." And yet at other times we may wonder how or why an all-powerful God would create puny, morally weak creatures like ourselves, put them in conditions of great struggle and hardship, and then punish them when they slip up. God made us the way we are. What purpose would it serve to punish such pitiable creatures? After all, God is omnipotent and beyond any possibility of harm from us. If God were to consider "extenuating circumstances," otherwise known as "the human condition,"—which he created—there might be no punishment at all. Under the circumstances, images of "hell-fire and brimstone" seem way beyond the pale and imply an unnecessarily harsh God.

Many of us hesitate to believe in this sort of God and would rather believe in a more merciful and forgiving deity. It makes more sense that God would want for his creatures to fulfill all the potential with which he endowed them. It seems more sensible if life were not a test which we can irretrievably fail but a training ground from which we can all continue to learn and grow. As a kind of parent, a creator should wish for his children to mature and increase in wisdom and self-knowledge. With death as an interim graduation, a loving and compassionate creator would fashion an afterlife to facilitate an ongoing growth of the soul. The role of God as punisher or administrator of justice would not bring this about. Such divine punishment would almost certainly block any possibility of personal growth, just as our jails rarely reform anyone and our executions no one.

And so we are down to this: a harsh, punishing God is not a worthy God, and yet, at the same time, how can we allow the bad to get off "scott-free?" For the evil to never suffer for their deeds is an appalling thought. Here I can suggest one possible solution. God does not punish us in the afterlife for our misdeeds; we punish ourselves. In our life here on earth, we may or may not feel remorse for our sins, and if we do, it is often of a thin and vacillating sort. There are too many obstacles which cloud our vision. We may not really understand the harm we've done, and if we do have a glimmer of it, there are usually endless excuses we can offer up to try to justify or rationalize our guilt. And, in fact, the psychological factors which caused us to commit the wrong in the first place may still be present. But in the afterlife, with all of our earthly needs and wants stripped away, the scales have been taken from our eyes, we can see clearly for the first time the harm we've done and also for the first time feel genuine remorse. In such remorse there is self-suffering and self-punishment, a kind of purging or "purgation," and so, therefore, a measure of justice. God is freed from the unbecoming task of meting out punishments. We punish ourselves and in our remorse are the seeds of self-knowledge. Remorse would seem to be the one emotion which most facilitates the growth of self-knowledge. Let this be our first clue to the nature of the afterlife.

The activities of philosophers and scientists are guided by the particular "problems" they're attempting to solve. In this case, we're trying to posit an afterlife which would give meaning to and be an extension of our earthly life. As we've already said, concepts like *nirvana* or the "beatific vision" are essentially non-sequiturs; they do not really lend meaning to our earthly lives. If anything, they appear to devalue it, as if to say that we live relatively meaningless lives on earth until we die, at which time everything suddenly becomes meaningful. What we're trying to do here is connect the two and show how one is preparation for the other.

Some of the criteria used by philosophers and scientists in the formulation of their theories express many of the elements of beauty. This includes such qualities as order, symmetry, proportion, coherence, elegance or grace, and as mentioned above, parsimony or the economy of expression. In other words, there is a belief that the truth and its expression have beauty. The last mentioned—economy of expression—is especially important. This essentially means that the fewer the variables employed in explanation, the better it is, the greater the explanatory power. The goal is to explain more with less. The fewer the variables, the more economical the theory is, and the greater its simplicity and elegance and beauty. In science, this rule is known as "Occam's Razor" named after William Occam (1285-1349) who asserted that the simplest explanation tends to be the best one. Many scientists feel that when this is the case, it is strong evidence of the correctness of the theory. This is similar to Newton's statement mentioned earlier that we should not ascribe more causes than necessary to explain natural events. If a theory or hypothesis has too many variables, it becomes unwieldy, nebulous, and overly complex. In other words, it loses its beauty, it becomes unseemly or "ugly."

The example frequently given for this sort of thing is the transition in astronomy from the ancient Ptolemaic model of the solar system to the Copernican. In the Ptolemaic model the Earth was at the center with the sun and planets revolving around it. Unfortunately, in this system the orbits of the planets and sun were incredibly complex and irregular, with the planets occasionally even reversing course. In contrast, the Copernican model with the sun at its center and all of the planets, including the Earth, circling around it, resulted in elegant and regular elliptical orbits. The simplicity and beauty of this model was a powerful clue of its correctness.

In our own case, we'll employ only one rather simple assumption or hypothesis, namely that in the afterlife we exist in some incorporeal form, which permits us to merge with other souls, to scan their life-memories and come to know them as they know themselves. This one assumption will allow us to make sense of such concepts as justice, forgiveness, mercy, goodness, beauty, etc., as we've said, and in a way which has tremendous explanatory power, particularly in giving meaning to our earthly lives as preparation for an afterlife.

Let's begin by supposing that when we die we live on in incorporeal fashion, that is, without a material body, in some form of energy, perhaps, as Dante describes the souls he encounters in the *Paradiso*, as "sheathes of living light" or "shining globes,"[120] or possibly, Milton's "spirits of purest light"[121] in *Paradise Lost.*[*] We retain the memories of our life to be reviewed or "scanned" as we wish, and now, with a clear vision unobstructed by earthly needs, we can learn all that there is to learn from our past life. We can learn from our failures, and from our successes as well. We would grow, accordingly, in self-knowledge and wisdom. But now what? It does not seem that the process is complete or that many of us would have achieved perfect wisdom from the life we'd led. As we saw in Part One, Socrates declared that if the individual soul does persist in the afterlife, he

---

[*] Plutarch, in his essay, "On the Delay of the Divine Vengeance," invents an interesting mythical afterlife. His souls, much like Dante's and Milton's, are "enveloped all around with light and translucent within," but some appear "mottled" or bruised, somewhat like an imperfect or flawed jewel, indicating past sins. See Plutarch's *Moralia*, Loeb Classical Library, Harvard University Press, Cambridge, Mass., 2000, Vol. VII, 564, p. 277.

would continue as he had done in his earthly life—continue his pursuit of truth and self-knowledge through an ongoing dialogue with other souls.

But how could this really occur? How could incorporeal bundles of energy interact in an incorporeal world? Would there be some sort of activity taking place? What would there be to do in a world where it was no longer necessary to attend to the needs of the body, to work for survival, to seek a mate and have children, etc. What would there possibly be *to do*? Surely not to "gaze at the face of God" for eternity. This in itself is a form of annihilation. And eternity is a long time. I've always felt that rather than thinking of the beatific vision as seeing the face of God, it would be better to see it as comprehending the mind of God, or comprehending God's "vision" of the world.

Let's assume that, as forms of energy, free from our bodies, we could now unite with one another in a way that had never been possible before. In our earthly lives we seek friendship and intimacy to whatever extent we are able, to communicate and get to know each other, to love one another, to unite our bodies, to share our lives. But our bodies get in the way of perfect knowledge of the other. Our bodies provide an insurmountable barrier to the complete melding of minds or souls. No matter how much we wish, we can never get completely inside the other person's mind. Even our attempt to unite our bodies only reminds us of the ultimate futility of seeking perfect union with each other.

Now, however, free from our bodies, we would be able for the first time to merge our souls together as one. Presumably, we would then have access to the other person's memory. We would be able to "scan" and see their lives through their own eyes and all their senses as they themselves had experienced it. During the time that we scanned or reviewed the other person's life, we would virtually be that person. Likewise, as they reviewed our life, they would become us for that time. The final result would be a new person, a new soul consisting of the lives and memories of two people. With the combined life memories of two lives, their new composite-soul would be wiser than either had been individually. The development and growth of self-knowledge for each would be facilitated by their union. They would literally be two-in-one. It would be one soul with two complete sets of lifetime memories. It is said that we all seek intimacy. What could be more intimate than this? We all seek love. What could be more loving than this?—to take on the entirety of another person's life, not just the good but the hardship also. We are reminded of the words of Paul of Tarsus: "For now we see through a glass darkly; but then face to face; now I know in part; but then I shall know even as also I am known."[122] Or as Seneca speculates on the afterlife: "There is no secrecy here, but minds are uncovered and hearts revealed and our lives are open and manifest to all."[123]

This process, of course, might continue, combining with other souls, adding to our life experiences and growing in self-knowledge as we form a new and greater group-soul. And yet, the individual souls would not be annihilated or lost in the new group soul, but would continue to persist or become immortal within that group-soul. Not only would the individual soul persist within the group-soul, but also the specific life memories it had experienced in its earthly existence. These would always be available for scanning or reliving by the individual or by any other soul who wished to review it. A day, a month, a year, or even an entire life of any member of the group soul could be relived at will. This sort of group-soul, I think, represents a kind of multiplication of being, a fuller and more abundant form of being than we experience in our earthly lives. Or as Dante describes his vision in the seventh sphere of heaven, "Before my eyes a hundred shining globes entwined their beams, soul adding grace to soul in Paradise."[124] And in Paradise Lost, Milton portrays a conversation between Adam, the first man, and the Angel Raphael. Adam asks Raphael how heavenly spirits communicate: "Bear with me, then, if lawful what I ask. Love not the Heavenly Spirits, and how their love express they, by looks only, or do they mix irradiance, virtual or immediate touch?" To which the angel answers:

> Let it suffice thee that thou know'st
> Us happy, and without Love no happiness,
> Whatever pure thou in the body enjoy'st
> (And pure thou wert created) we enjoy
> In eminence, and obstacle find none
> Of membrane, joint, limb, exclusive bars;
> Easier than air with air, if Spirits embrace,
> Total they mix, union of pure with pure.[125]

It's interesting to note here that this process could actually be seen as a form of reincarnation. Every time we scanned another's life we would live it firsthand. It would be as if we were back on earth for that duration. This isn't identical, though, to the Hindu or Buddhist concept of reincarnation, where the individual soul is believed to be reborn as new individuals in time, rather than scanning the lives of those who have already lived and passed on. In the Buddhist system, the individual has no memory of their previous life, but what I am suggesting is that upon merging, each soul would come completely into possession of the other's memories. This really is the only way in which growth could take place. If there is forgetfulness between lives, there will be no growth. In the Eastern tradition, there is no mention of group-souls or of the wisdom and enlightenment gained in their formation. And, in any case, the goal for that tradition is to escape *samsara* or the endless cycle of death and rebirth.

Another fascinating idea arises here. We spoke earlier of the very natural desire that there should be justice in this world. For those for whom the sense of remorse in the afterlife is not punishment enough, we now have the potential for total and perfect justice. This occurs when a former harm-doer unites with his or her former "victim." A simple example would be that if you, in your earthly existence, had been a rotten husband —physically abusive, unfaithful, etc.—and were to combine with your wife in the afterlife, you would experience your own cruelty first-hand, through her eyes. The roles would be reversed, you would now be the victim. This would also be true, of course, if you were a terrible parent or friend, or for that matter, if you were in general an unkind stranger to everyone you met. We can even imagine that a political tyrant might be led to experience first-hand the misery and suffering he had caused to his subjects. And yet, in all of this, in experiencing our faults through the eyes of those who had been most subject to them, we would maximize our own growth in self-knowledge and wisdom. We would understand the wrong we had done in the clearest possible light. Here we have arrived at a wonderful combination of perfect justice *and* the growth of the soul.

This solves the problem, not just of combining justice with growth, but also the perennial difficulty of trying to match the punishment to the crime. Most concepts of reincarnation attempt to accomplish this by having the evil-doer reborn in more lowly and difficult circumstances, or even, in some schemes, reborn as an animal. This sort of thing might constitute punishment, but trying to calibrate the transmigration of the soul in such a way as to perfectly match the crime approaches absurdity. This is the inherent problem with concepts like "*karma.*" Such solutions still only approximate justice at best. Beyond the question of "extenuating circumstances," keeping a strict accounting of such "sins" and their punishments extended over many generations is beyond all reason. Such crimes are ultimately too indeterminate. It can probably be said that each crime is unique, committed by unique individuals, under unique circumstances. This makes the problem of perfectly tailoring the punishment to the crime essentially unsolvable within such concepts of reincarnation.

Plato, in the *Laws*, presents a concept of reincarnation which moves beyond simply having the individual reborn into different circumstances or as a lower creature by having them suffer nearly the same crime they had committed in their previous life. He writes: "Vengeance is exacted for these crimes in the afterlife, and when a man returns to this world again he is ineluctably obliged . . . to undergo the same treatment as he himself meted out to his victim, and to conclude his earthly existence by encountering a similar fate at the hands of someone else."[126] Plato is willing to give examples: "If ever a man murdered his father, in the course of time he must suffer the same fate from violent treatment at the hands of his children. A matricide, before being reborn, must adopt the female sex, and after being born a woman and bearing children, be dispatched subsequently by them."[127] Of course, the horrific consequence of Plato's scheme of reincarnation is that rather than generating justice, it appears to create the conditions for generating endless subsequent crimes. Someone committing patricide or matricide must in turn be murdered by their own children in their next life, but then presumably their children will also have to be murdered by their own children, and so on *ad infinitum*.

Even in terms of Plato's attempt to create a perfect match between crime and punishment, the weakness of his solution can be seen in his statement that the reincarnated evil-doer must suffer, "*a similar fate at the hands of someone else.*" This fate is merely similar rather than precise, and this is so at least in part because the new crime which it generates is committed by someone else.

All of this expresses the *perfect symmetry* of the solution provided in the "scanning" process when the soul of one harm-doer scans and relives the life of the person he formerly harmed. As stated earlier, he now experiences the crime as its victim, indeed, as the victim of himself. There is no new crime or criminal generated. The suffering experienced is precise in every way to that experienced by his former victim, and the evil or harmfulness of his act will now be seen by him with perfect clarity. This gives new meaning to the biblical saying that we should do unto others as we would have others do unto us, since in this case any harm or benefit we had done to others will now come back to us with perfect precision. Most importantly, however, is that this makes possible the genuine remorse and growth of the soul of the harm-doer.

This perfect symmetry is one of our components of beauty. It's interesting that symmetry is not only an important element in aesthetics, but in science as well, particularly physics. Brian Greene writes in *The Elegant Universe*: "Physicists describe these properties as symmetries of nature . . . Much in the same manner that they affect art and music, such symmetries are deeply satisfying; they highlight an order and a coherence in the workings of nature. The elegance of rich, complex, and diverse phenomena emerging from a simple set of universal laws is at least part of what physicists mean when they invoke the term 'beautiful.'"[128] It might be added that in this case we not only have perfect symmetry between harm-doer and harmed, constituting perfect justice, but we also have proportion, that is, the crime and the punishment match each other perfectly, they are a perfect fit, and this proportion is another of our elements of beauty.

On the more positive side, we could, by the same token, experience the effects of any love or kindness we had shown in our life, or of good works we had done. Again, it is fair or just that we do so. Such considerations lead us to speculate on who we would choose to "merge" with in our afterlife. If the goal is maximum growth, then merging with our immediate family would probably be the most productive since these are the people we had been in closest contact with, and this would allow us to see ourself close-up from their perspective. In this way we could not avoid seeing our faults and weaknesses from the other's viewpoint, and, of course, our strengths and virtues also. It could be a painful process but one most likely to lead to a growth in wisdom. The group-soul formed in this case would be of a special kind—a family-group-soul.

This could mean merging with our spouses and our children (when they, too, pass away). It could also mean merging with our parents. Many of us are quick to place blame with our parents for our own faults and weaknesses. By joining with them we'd often see more clearly the reasons for their actions as parents, and occasionally that we ourselves weren't always ideal children. In any event, to understand our parents better, we might even go so far as to merge with *their* parents (our grandparents). It isn't hard to see that if continued on, this process leads backwards to an ever widening circle of souls, extending out gradually to the human family as a whole.

In this way, our life in the hereafter wouldn't constitute a radical break with our earthly lives. Instead, it would build upon it. Kant tells us that in the afterlife, "Man has no ground for believing that a sudden change will take place. Rather, experience of his state on earth and the ordering of nature in general gives him clear proofs that his . . . moral improvement and the well-being resulting therefrom, will continue endlessly, ie., eternally."[129]

Earlier we mentioned that the concept of reincarnation in Eastern religion (Hinduism, Buddhism) excludes the carry-over of memories from life to life. This was also the case in ancient Greek mythology wherein the deceased must travel the River Lethe on their way to Hades, the underworld abode of the dead. "Lethe," in Greek, means "forgetfulness." Upon traveling the River Lethe all memory of their former life is erased. Once again, I think we would have to reject this concept, in both the Greek and Oriental versions, as it appears to preclude the opportunity for growth. In the scanning of other's lives during the merging process in the afterlife, we would be able to retain all of the memories not only of our own original life, but of everyone we had merged with.

And yet it is possible that even though no memories would be lost, there might be a gradual distancing process as we absorbed the life-memories of more and more people. The intensity of the emotions which accompanied these memories, including those which were painful, would begin to diminish over time. Our attachment to our own original earthly existence might begin to fade somewhat as we grew as a composite-soul. We would perceive the events of our former life from a much greater perspective of understanding and wisdom. This would apply to all of the lives we had scanned. Who do we really become at this point, when our original life is just one among many? On the one hand our soul is enormously augmented in wisdom and knowledge as we take in the memories of others, but at the same time we may begin to let go of a strong attachment or identification with any particular identity, even our original one. Eventually we might simply begin to feel like an actor who had played many parts. The aesthetic element, or the element of beauty, begins to arise here, but this would depend upon progress in our ability to incorporate truth and goodness.

I think it's important to see this merging process as *voluntary*. No souls would merge except as they freely will to do so. All unions must be voluntary; otherwise, it would be a form of rape, or forced intimacy. Each soul would progress at their own pace when they felt ready to do so. However, the individual soul has great motivation to merge with those who are most likely to further their growth in wisdom.

We may not choose to merge with family members, but with others instead. Beyond our family, who would we wish to unite with? To unite with friends would no doubt teach us a lot about ourselves, and much of it would be a positive experience. From the standpoint of growth, however, we might actually learn more by merging with our enemies. Plutarch asks in his essay, "How to Profit by One's Enemies," "What is to hinder a man from taking his enemy as his teacher, and profiting thereby, and thus learning, to some extent, the things of which he was unaware? For there are many things an enemy is quicker to perceive than a friend."[130] In other words, an enemy will tell us the hard truth about ourself, while friends are reluctant to do so. Two mutual enemies merging with each other would put both on the receiving end of the more objectionable aspects of their own personalities. If there had been a misunderstanding, which is so often the case in such animosities, all would now be made clear. And, in truth, all enmities are based upon misunderstanding of a kind, in the sense that we are generally unaware of the psychology and background of the person we believe has wronged us. This, again, would now be revealed as we experienced the other's life and all of the negative experiences which may have contributed to their actions. Each would now have all of the other person's lifetime memories with all of their fears and hopes, and failures and successes. To hate the other now would be to hate themselves. But this is no longer likely.

We may possibly wish to merge with people (if they're willing) whom we had never known in our lifetime. Although here we would not have the opportunity to see ourself as others had seen us in our former life, we may still benefit from the life experiences of the other person. Naturally, there might be a tendency to wish to unite only with the rich and famous and powerful, and those who had led charmed lives generally, and this is understandable. We learn not only from failures but successes also. It's important to understand not just all of the bad things that can happen in life but all the good things too. Perhaps the most instructive lives, though, would be those who had risen to great success after overcoming hardship. This would allow us to experience true success and the character it requires.

In the *Apology*, Socrates talks about who he would like to communicate with in heaven. As someone who was himself tried and sentenced to death unfairly, he says that it would be "rather amusing" to meet Palamedes and Ajax the son of Telamon and any other heroes of the old days who met their death through an unfair trial. Following the argument we're making here, he might have done well to merge or "commune" with his accusers. Only then would they begin to understand the magnitude of their crime. More importantly, though, Socrates tells us that he would like to converse with the great minds of the past. "How much would one give to meet Orpheus and Musaeus, Hesiod and Homer? I am willing to die ten times over if this is possible . . . Above all I should like to spend my time there, as here, in examining and searching people's minds, to find out who is really wise among them. What would one not give to be able to question the leader of that great host against Troy, or Odysseus, or Sisyphus or the thousands of other men and women whom one could mention, to talk and mix and argue with whom would be unimaginable happiness."[131]

For the philosopher, and ultimately for all of us, the goal is knowledge. The German philosopher, Friedrich Nietzsche, expressed this yearning in one of his books: "The sigh of the search for knowledge—'Oh my greed! There is no selflessness in my soul but only an all coveting self that would like to appropriate many individuals as so many additional pairs of eyes and hands—a self that would like to bring back the whole past, too, and that will not lose anything that it could possibly possess . . . Oh, that I might be reborn in a hundred beings! . . . Whoever does not know this sigh from firsthand experience does not know the passion of the search for knowledge."[132]

When you think about it, we often try to approximate something like this scanning process in our earthly lives. We read biographies of people we admire or we may live another person's life vicariously when we identify with a character in a movie or play or novel. We do so, on the one hand, for fun or play, but on the other, we often find it to be instructional, when we can learn something about life, whether the characters are fictional or real. Now in the afterlife the identification is no longer vicarious, but immediate and firsthand.

In the tenth book of the *Republic*, Plato relates the myth of Er, a warrior who is thought to be dead, but who, after witnessing the afterlife, revives to tell everyone what he saw. Er claimed that he witnessed a "strange, pitiful, and ridiculous scene" wherein those who had died were free to choose their next life. A countless variety of lives were spread out before them from which to choose. Unlike the concept of reincarnation in Eastern religion, their choice was not determined by *karma* or the deeds of their past life. They were free to choose according to the limits of their own wisdom or foolishness. Some, for example, attracted by power, snatched up the life of a tyrant. These, according to Plato, were doomed to misery, unaware of the hellish lives of most tyrants, who must always fear for their lives, even to the point of destroying everyone close to them who may be a threat to their power. Strangely enough, writes Plato, those who made the wisest choices were those who had experienced suffering in their past life. These, "since they had themselves suffered, and seen the sufferings of others, did not make their choices precipitously."[133] Particularly commendable was the soul of Odysseus who, "from memory of its former toils flung away ambition and went about for a long time in quest of the relatively carefree life of an ordinary citizen, who minded his own business, and with difficulty found it lying in some corner disregarded by the others."[134]

In time, all of these unions would form a new "group-soul"—an entity much more powerful, wiser, compassionate and embracing than any single individual soul could be. But are there souls whom we would not wish to scan, or, so to speak, "reincarnate?" What about someone who had led a completely despicable life, such as a child killer? Few of us would want to review or relive such a life. It's difficult to see what we would have to gain by doing so. There are a few possible solutions here. First, if no one wished to merge with such a soul, it would remain fallow. No one would scan it. And in fact, given a choice, such a person would probably not wish to relive their own life. It would never be "reincarnated." Socrates mentions this possibility in the *Phaedo*: "The soul which is impure . . . By setting its hand to lawless bloodshed or committing other kindred crimes . . . This soul is shunned and avoided by all; none will company with it or guide it, and it wanders alone in utter desolation."[135] This in itself would serve as the ultimate punishment for its deeds. This solution might seem to be a form of justice in earthly terms, but it may be too harsh from our higher standpoint of love, mercy, and compassion, and we should perhaps reject it on that account.

Another solution might be to allow for the possibility of "one-way" scanning. In this case, the wretched soul could receive the memories of the life experiences of others but would not impart their own to them. They might receive healing and a deeper understanding from the life experience of the other person without inflicting their own horrid memories on them. Perhaps this could be a prerequisite to joining the larger group soul. When they had finally reached a level of wisdom from scanning the lives of others, they might be allowed to merge with the group soul. But a more elegant and economical and merciful and just solution is to assume that the process of soul-merging has been going on since the beginning of time in the formation of a group-soul comprised of the souls of everyone who had ever lived and died, and that such a vast soul would have more than the needed strength, compassion, and goodness to absorb such an afflicted soul without any harm to itself.

At this point, some readers may have felt objection to the seeming tediousness of living so many different lives in the process of merging with other souls. An average life-span of seventy-plus years may seem long to the person living it. On the other hand, I believe that most of us, when arriving at the end of our lives realize that in an eternity of time life is just a brief flash. It's also possible, I think, that when we scan another person's life, it happens in a much quicker way than if we were living it out in "real time." It may be a little like scanning a video on fast-forward. People who have been near death sometimes say that their entire life flashed before them in just a brief moment. It might be something like this when we scan another person's life. At the end of the process we've absorbed all of their memories.

One other variation here is to suppose that it may be possible to simply take on another's memories, available for recall, without having to completely scan the other's life sequentially from beginning to end. This would also solve the problem, not only of the good having to relive the lives of the bad, but also of geniuses having to relive the lives of the dull or obtuse.

Having gone this far, we might as well add that the possibility of taking on another's memories without having to fully review their life also offers a solution to the question of what happens to animals in the afterlife. On the one hand, it seems asinine to assume that when a dog or cat dies, its soul is condemned to continue at the same level of existence for eternity in the afterlife. If the animal becomes "enlightened" in the afterlife, for example, by partaking of the life memories of higher creatures such as humans it would no longer be a dog or cat, etc.; it would be a higher form of being. If it were unable to undergo this process, then it would be condemned to live in the darkness of its former existence. We should also avoid the presumption that while we humans have immortal souls, other creatures have none at all. The more relevant question is probably whether they have memories. If so, then we should allow for the possibility that when such creatures die, the energy or life-force of their souls are added to the group soul along with whatever memories they have, if any at all. Their memories would be available for recall by others who might be curious about such things, without each of us having to relive the entire lives of every dog or cat or dragonfly or worm that ever lived. And the souls of those simple creatures which have no memories, but functioned solely by instinct, would contribute their life-force to the group-soul but could not be reviewed or "reincarnated."

But perhaps we've said too much too quickly here. It may be better if we back up a little and assume for the moment that when we die, we do not immediately take on the memories of every human and creature to have ever existed but that we do so only one at a time and with those with whom we freely choose to merge. If we see it this way, I believe our understanding of the meaning of it all will be clearer. We should even assume that we do scan the entire life of each individual we unite with, or at least that we have the choice of doing so. After all, simply recalling disjointed memories of another person's life may not be very instructive when out of context of their life as a whole.

Once again, although I've used the word "reincarnation" several times, this should not be equated with the Buddhist or Hindu concept. First, there is no "*karma*" involved; second, in the Eastern concept the individual soul goes from one life to another, one by one in a linear sequence extending forward in time, distinct and separate from the sequence of any other soul. Also, there is no merging; the lives are discretely separated in time. In my own concept, there is extensive overlap in the scanning and merging of souls, perhaps, even, in an eternity of time, the merging of all souls with one another. This would include living the life of, or "reincarnating" as someone from the distant past if we chose. I sometimes even suspect that the afterlife is beyond sequential time and that the souls of everyone who had ever lived in the past and will ever live in the future are present to us for scanning. From this all-encompassing perspective, a godlike being could "dip down" and experience at will the life—or perhaps any shorter interval, a year, a day, etc.—of any individual to have ever lived. In Part

One we spoke of the deep mystery of self-identity. Why are we who we are and not someone else? Why weren't we born into another body, in another time and place? Now, in the afterlife, it would virtually be possible to be anyone who had ever lived, to experience their lives as they has experienced it.

Finally, the Hindu/Buddhist also believes that the goal of all of these incarnations is to *not* have to continue to do so and to escape or transcend all such things into a state of *nirvana* or *moksha*, an indescribable condition of bliss. But as we've said, this sort of vague formulation is a non-sequitur and is not really a "solution" at all to the problem we're trying to solve. It doesn't show in what way the afterlife can help us make sense of our earthly lives. In what follows I'll offer a more exciting alternative.

Chapter 7

Truth, Goodness, and Beauty

We've granted that the purpose behind all of this "merging" is to promote greater self-knowledge and wisdom for each soul involved. But there is an enormous question remaining—the growth of self-knowledge and wisdom to what end? Two or three or more souls merge together and grow accordingly, but then what? We are back to our original question about the afterlife. What do we actually *do* there, with our new-found wisdom?

There are two possible answers to this question, the first of which I must reject. The first is that we use our new wisdom as a kind of ministering spirit or "angel," helping those still in their earthly existence. However attractive this idea is, I just don't see it. If there are millions or even billions of angels or ministering spirits on the other side, consisting of all the souls who have passed before, available to assist us here on earth, the benefits are not evident. Beyond this, such well-intentioned assistance, if it did occur, might actually interfere with the playing out of the individual's destiny.

There is a more plausible and exciting explanation for what we do in the afterlife with our new wisdom, but before we answer this question, we need to first try to resolve another philosophical dilemma. Just as in attempting to reconcile the opposing concepts of a sternly just God with a loving, merciful God, we were led to the resolution that we punish ourselves through genuine, undiluted remorse in the afterlife, so we may also make progress in our understanding here if we are able to resolve three distinct explanations sometimes offered for the "meaning" of life. These can be referred to as the philosophical, the ethical, and the aesthetic. Each of these, it will be noticed, correspond to one of the three ideals we've mentioned so frequently in this book, truth (the philosophical), goodness (the ethical), and beauty (the aesthetic). These three do not always seem to be perfectly compatible. To give just one example, the view that goodness

84

or doing good is the most important thing in life can sometimes appear to be at odds with the view that beauty or the creation of beauty is paramount. The first is very serious about life; the second somewhat playful. To be able to synthesize these three ideals, both practically and conceptually, could become a strong foundation and guide for infusing meaning into both our earthly lives and an afterlife.

The first two, the philosophic and the ethical, I believe, have already been united in the Socratic teaching that the pursuit of truth, particularly in the form of self-knowledge, is the basis of integrity and moral strength. For Socrates, life is a kind of training ground for the growth of the soul. This view, however, as already suggested, comes into conflict with the "aesthetic" view, which can be found, for example, in some schools of Eastern religion, such as the Hindu or Taoist concept that existence is *lila* or the "play" of god—in other words, that existence is essentially playful.

The view that the purpose behind existence is play maintains that existence must be perfect as it is. Play is the only activity which is good solely in itself. It is non-teleological, or rather, its end or *telos* is contained within itself. Because it is nonteleological, its focus is on the present and not on some future, unrealized state. When children play, for example, they are completely absorbed in the present moment, in the "now." During that time, they are in need of nothing, they are in a perfect joyous state in a kind of self-contained world, perhaps something like that of the fabled Adam and Eve before their expulsion from paradise. Thus, for existence to be perfect, it must in some higher sense be "playful." The philosopher, Nietzsche, said that, "Only as an aesthetic product can the world be justified for all eternity."[136] This is Nietzsche's answer to the first question of philosophy, "Why does anything exist at all? Why not nothingness?" For Nietzsche, the only justification for existence is aesthetic, that is, when its purpose is beauty. And the essential nature of beauty is play.*

---

* See, for example, Friedrich Schiller's *On the Aesthetic Education of Man*, particularly the Fifteenth Letter. Schiller writes: "We shall never be wrong in seeking a man's ideal of Beauty along the selfsame path in which he satisfies his play impulse . . . Man shall *only play* with Beauty, and he shall play *only with Beauty.*" Notice in the arts, for instance, we "play" music, in the theater we go to "plays," in the visual arts we have the play of color and form and line, etc.

To begin with, this view offers a solution to the problem of suffering in the world in a very interesting way. On a philosophical level, one of the reasons the existence of suffering is such a difficult problem is that it appears to reflect on the very nature of the universe. If there is suffering or evil in the world, and God created the world, then isn't God an imperfect creator? More simply, if creation is flawed, then the creator must also be flawed. Or so it seems.

Eastern religion solves this difficulty by holding that "polarity" is central to all existence. The world is divided into opposites: positive/negative, full/empty, hot/cold, light/dark, male/female, pleasure/pain, good/evil, and on and on. Indeed, the existence of one end of the "pole" implies its opposite—hot implies cold, light implies dark, good implies evil. Each can only be defined with reference to its opposite. "Good" could have no meaning if there were no such thing as "not-good." Behind the apparent duality there is an underlying unity. Thus, existence, in this tradition, is the interaction or play of these opposites.

Yet, how can we call "play" something which includes suffering and pain? It is instructive in this regard to look at what people themselves consider to be play. When we play a game, we have the interaction again of opposites. Our opponent is, for the moment at least, the "bad" guy, and we, of course, are the "good" guy. The pleasure comes, for the duration of the game, from pretending it to be important or "real" in some sense, though we know deep down that it is "only a game." In our recreation, we re-create, on the level of play, the "real" drama of life.

If we examine our other playful or recreational activities, again we derive pleasure from watching dramas (or "plays") which depict the eternal struggle between the forces of good and evil. Whether in novels or movies or on stage, we "suspend disbelief" and imagine that the drama is real. In all play there is pretending. We pretend our games are important or real. In enjoying drama we pretend that it is really happening. We identify with or pretend to be the hero or heroine. The child pretends in his play to be Spiderman or James Bond or some other superhero. The real meaning of it all is not the victory of one "pole" over the other, but in the play between the two. And indeed, the very fact that we enjoy watching or acting out this interaction is a clue to the truth of this.

But this perspective appears to undermine the Socratic view that the meaning of life is in the care of our souls, in the growth of self-knowledge and moral strength. This concept of growth is teleological, it is growth toward some higher end. In this case, the higher end is wisdom or moral perfection. In this view, morality is taken very seriously, which seems to bring it into conflict with the view that existence is play. If life is play, what is the value in being moral? The victory of good over evil seems to lose much of its significance if it is just part of the playing out of some cosmic drama. In the Eastern tradition, it's held that good should not expect to vanquish bad, but must learn to co-exist with it as a necessary part of *lila*, the play of God.

If all of this talk of Eastern religion sounds remote or foreign to Western ears, it's useful to remember that Plato, the founder of Western philosophy, states in Book IV of *The Laws*: "Of course, the affairs of human beings are not worthy of great seriousness; yet it is necessary to be serious about them . . . What is human has been devised as a certain plaything of god, and that this is really the best thing about it. Every man and woman should spend life in this way, playing the noblest possible games, and thinking about them in a way that is opposite of the way they're now thought about."[137] Notice that Plato speaks of playing "the noblest" possible games. Plato's writings as a whole indicate that for him the noblest game or the highest form of creativity or play are those which are guided by goodness and truth. The pursuit of truth, in particular, could be regarded as a form of play or "game" resembling "hide-and-seek," where the truth hides and we seek to discover or uncover it. Any good scientist or philosopher will tell you that their search for truth and knowledge is a great adventure. These truth-seekers ask questions which send them on "quests" for the answers. Like pirates searching for buried treasure or Knights of the Round Table hunting for the Holy Grail or Jason pursuing the Golden Fleece, scientists and philosophers seek the truth, which, for them, is like all three rolled into one.

We should consider the possibility here that there may be levels of play. The reader of a book or the member of an audience watching a drama becomes a participant vicariously, but I believe the author who writes the drama, the composer who writes the music, the artist who paints the painting, are all "playing" at a higher level. They are *creating worlds*. Creativity, then, becomes the highest form of play as expressed in art of all kinds. And it may be, in a sense, in the afterlife we become *both* the play-write *and* an actor in our play. But such creativity must be, in Plato's terms, "noble." It must be guided by truth and goodness and beauty. And of these three, truth must come first, since there can be no goodness without truth, and no beauty without truth and goodness.

We are ready to answer the question of what we actually do in the afterlife. After combining with other souls we grow in wisdom and knowledge but what do we do with all of this wisdom and knowledge? I believe the answer is this: we *dream together*. We create new worlds together. Each identity in the group soul plays a part in the dream, but now with the combined memories of all the other souls. Think of it this way: In our earthly lives, when we sleep and dream, each character in our dream is actually just a projection of ourself. If one of these characters says something in the dream, it is we who put the words into their mouth. They do whatever we make them do, even if it might be said that we do so at a very subconscious level. These dreams may be pleasant or painful, even nightmarish, depending perhaps on the level of unresolved tensions in our psyche. These dreams are often very fleeting and phantomlike and upon awakening can barely be remembered.

But in the dream of a group-soul it would be quite different. Each member of the group-soul would play their own part and yet still have the combined memory and knowledge of the whole. Each character in the dream would have its own separate identity or "reality" rather than being a projection of a single dreamer. Because of this, and because of the combined energy or life-force of the group, the dream itself would take on a whole new level of reality, unlike our earthly dreams. Such dreams could become very beautiful and real according to the level of wisdom and the amount of life-energy or number of souls in the new group-soul. Unlike Shakespeare's Hamlet who fears, "what dreams may come," there would no longer be nightmares—such dreams would likely be filled with light, joy, and beauty.

To create a world and then play in it. This type of creativity is certainly the highest form of play conceivable. And the element of morality is not lost. Indeed, the beauty of the group dream will depend in large part on the combined level of moral wisdom of its members. It seems reasonable to assume that such a group soul may even seek out those to join it who are most likely to contribute in this regard. The person, who, in their life on earth suffered hardships and yet overcame them to become generous and loving would be a valued addition to the group. Everyone in the group would benefit from reviewing such a person's life and the group dream would take on a new grace and beauty.

The creative people, the artists, will also make a great contribution to the collective dream. They were the creators of worlds in their earthly lives and will help assure that the group dream will be rich in beauty and elegance. Even the bon-vivant, the sensuous or creative person, the lover of beauty, who knew how to affirm life's pleasures, will have a role to play, for I am assuming that in this composite dream everyone will have "bodies"—projected from their imaginations like every other physical manifestation in their dream—and that through the power of scanning or perfect recollection will be able to recreate the experience of the sensual. This will be a much higher expression of *eros*, however, in the perfect union of both body and soul. Such an existence in the afterlife would combine the playful, the aesthetic or creative, with the growth of the soul. Thus our earthly lives would have been a kind of "dress rehearsal" for the afterlife, thereby infusing meaning into both. It may be that in this creative power manifested in the afterlife we have the highest expression of the biblical saying that we are made in the image of God, the Creator.

What are the roles of truth, goodness, and beauty in the afterlife? As for truth, the pursuit continues in our merging with and learning from others. What of goodness? Could merged souls still harm each other in such an afterlife? Perhaps, but I believe they would not. Certainly, their newfound wisdom would point them away from any need for harming others. And more importantly, when you know the other as you know yourself, you would have no motive to do harm. As two souls in one, to harm the other would be to harm yourself.

Is it possible that a group soul might choose to dream an adventure where risks could be taken, or a drama enacting the perennial struggle between good and evil? Perhaps, but the first important difference here from our earthly lives is that the members of the group soul would be aware that it was a dream and so still be in the nature of play. It would be like the pleasure we get from watching a drama, when we suspend disbelief and yet know that it is not entirely real, and in this case, there would be the added pleasure of having helped to "author" the drama. But without this awareness that it is "pretend," it would not be play, but suffering. This is the main argument against seeing our earthly lives as a group dream, as some have said. My own guess is that while a group soul might choose such a dream-narrative, they would be much more likely to find that they had already had their fill of such drama in their earthly lives, and would prefer to skip directly to the happy ending, so to speak, where everyone lived happily ever-after.

Or we might think of it this way. If we break goodness down into three categories: first, not causing suffering; second, the relief of suffering; and third, the giving of pleasure, then in the afterlife, not causing suffering will become far less important since there will be little occasion or motivation to do so; the relief of suffering will have some importance and may take place through the merging and "rewriting" or atonement process we'll discuss later; and the giving of pleasure to others will now become the most important expression of goodness. This moves goodness into the realm of the aesthetic. Goodness, in this case, will consist primarily in gift-giving. The gift of truth and knowledge edifies and heals. The gift of beauty inspires and brings joy. We'll be surrounded with pure good-will. In books that have studied the experience of people who have died and been resuscitated, many reported that in their brief glimpse of the afterlife, it was is if the air "vibrated with love." It may be, as Dante tells us, "that all things spring from love in Paradise."[138] And elsewhere he writes, "As mirror reflects mirror, so, above, the more there are who join their souls, the more love learns perfection, and the more they love."[139]

In other words, goodness, if anything, would now express itself primarily in a purely positive form as the giving of pleasure which would be an expression of "love." In part, as we've already seen, this pleasure or love would consist in imparting whatever knowledge and wisdom we might be able to impart, as all members of the group soul become both teachers and pupils of one another. Beyond this, however, this pleasure would increasingly become preoccupied with the creation and appreciation of beauty, as all members also become both artists and spectators of one another's creations. Along this line, Santayana writes in *The Sense of Beauty* that, "If we attempt to remove from life all its evils, as the popular mind has done at times, we should find little but aesthetic pleasures remaining to constitute unalloyed happiness."[140]

Santayana's conjecture now appears to apply to the afterlife. In a heaven where all truth and knowledge is eventually known, and all suffering eliminated, beauty or the "aesthetic" now takes ascendance. In a world where our dreams become reality, creativity becomes paramount. Beauty may be expressed in the play of graceful narratives in which we ourselves are the actors, or it may take form in the fashioning of a surpassingly beautiful dream world. Perhaps one soul may be able to give pleasure to another by creating dreamlike "interludes," scenes and settings, dreamscapes, etc., like paintings that can be stepped into. At this point, beauty and goodness begin to converge, when goodness no longer consists only in the removal of suffering, but the giving of pleasure, which now takes the form of beauty and play. Or possibly we might share special moments from our past life, from our own personal treasure chest of memories.

More and more, the ultimate goal may become bliss—the complete absorption in beauty. Here, one is reminded of the biblical "beatific vision" but, I think, this vision as it is usually understood is too passive. In our group dream the members would be *creating* the beauty they perceive and this would include beauty as "playful" living. Most importantly, such beauty would be guided by and infused with truth and goodness. My own guess is that humor and laughter would play a large role. Humor is rare in that it expresses truth, goodness, and beauty all at once. Humor partakes of truth in dispelling pretense and presumption, which so often hide the truth; it partakes of goodness in spreading cheer and relieving suffering; and it participates in beauty in its playfulness and in the overflowing spirit expressed in laughter.

We should all imagine ourselves reaching the pearly gates and being asked the questions, "What do you have to contribute to the group soul? In what way can you enhance it or make it morally or aesthetically richer?" Most of all, will the narrative of your life be edifying to others when reviewed? If you were a mindless, conforming automaton in life, a clone of the lowest common denominator of human nature, then you will have little to contribute. This is why, in our earthly life, individualism is so important. It is similar to the practical advice we might give to a lonely person seeking friendship. What do you have to offer to a friendship, what do you bring to it? What do you have to *share* with another person? Do you have interesting pursuits, talents, knowledge, to share? Have you developed a good sense of humor? Are you an especially loving or compassionate person? In other words, have you cultivated your potential in life to the fullest?

My point here is that even though the concept of merging may seem to imply, as it has so often in various forms of mysticism, that the individual becomes little more than an aspect or reflection of the total, in truth, the more they had cultivated their individuality in life, the more they can contribute in the afterlife. The proper preparation for death is not a life of detachment or the stripping away of all of the things that make someone an individual, but rather cultivating, as a unique individual, the fullest excellence of character. Excellence can't be achieved through uniformity; to "excel" means to "go beyond"—this is a basic tenet of individualism. Too great an emphasis on individualism in our earthly lives is sometimes criticized for being a cover for selfishness or self-centeredness, which, unfortunately, is often true. But the insight behind holding self-realization in high regard is the importance for all humans to unleash their creative potential, both in life and in preparation for the afterlife.

I like the way that C.S. Lewis expresses it in his chapter on "Heaven" in *The Problem of Pain*: God "makes each soul unique. If He had no use for all these differences, I do not see why he should have created more souls than one . . . Your soul has a curious shape because it is a hollow made to fit particular swelling in the infinite contours of the Divine substance, or a key to unlock one of the doors in the house with many mansions . . . Your place in heaven will seem to be made for you and you alone, because you were made for it—made for it stitch by stitch as a glove is made for a hand . . . For doubtless the continually successful, yet never complete attempt by each soul to communicate its unique vision to all others (of which earthly art and philosophy are but clumsy imitations) is also among the ends for which the individual was created . . . As to its fellow creatures, each soul, we suppose, will be eternally engaged in giving away to all the rest that which it receives."[141]

There is a short poem by the Indian poet, Rabindranath Tagore, which conveys this nicely.

What Will You Give?

What will you give?
When death knocks at your door?

The fullness of my life—
The sweet wine of autumn days and summer nights,
My little hoard gleaned through the years,
And hours rich with living.

These will be my gift.
When death knocks at my door.

All of this argues in favor of a healthy individualism and the pursuit of excellence in truth, goodness, and beauty in our earthly lives. Those who had led noble and exemplary lives will have the most to contribute in the afterlife. Individuals who had done great harm to others in their lives, if allowed to merge with other souls, might not be permitted to take roles in these group dreams, which could constitute another form of punishment, or perhaps they could take on "rehabilitated" roles, acting from the standpoint of their newfound wisdom. A novel idea here would be for them to take an extremely giving role in the dream toward individuals they had formerly harmed as a sort of recompense.

It would be nice to think that with our new level of understanding in the afterlife we would not just feel remorse for any harm we'd done, but actually be able to do something to rectify it. Plutarch writes: "The thought that the soul of every wicked man revolves within itself and dwells upon is this: how it might escape from the memory of its inequities, drive out of itself the consciousness of guilt, regain its purity, and begin its life anew."[142] In the afterlife we've envisioned here, this now seems possible. If we're able to scan our lives and see clearly the individual instances of harm, whether large or small, we might go to the person who had received the harm and offer to recreate that experience with them in a wholly different manner, substituting praise for insult, friendship for animosity, helpfulness for harmfulness. In a manner of speaking, we could help to rewrite that part of their life, to rewrite their memories, replacing a painful experience with a joyful one. We could help create a new memory wherein we treated them with respect, love, compassion, whatever was most appropriate to counteract the harm we'd done. Scanning our lives we might do this with everyone we felt ourself to have acted poorly towards, offering each a new experience and memory to substitute for the old. And in the act of helping them to rewrite their past lives, we would be rewriting our own.

Just as in our earthly lives and in most versions of the afterlife, perfect justice is never attained but only some poor approximation to it, the same might be said of the potential for "atonement" or repair of the damage done, and for "redemption" or repair of oneself. As we've seen, when a harm-doer merges with someone he's harmed and relives the moment through the other's eyes, he now suffers the same precise harm and perfect justice is attained. And now if the possibility is available for each of us to rewrite regrettable incidents with others by recreating them in a wholly positive way, the path is opened not just for a rough equivalence to atonement and redemption but for their perfection.

This would be especially true if the "rewriting" or creation of a new narrative didn't simply add on a new version of the original incident, but in some way replaced it. One corollary of justice, after all, is to allow the harm-doer the chance to make amends or pay back the victim for the harm done. This is rarely possible in our earthly lives or in most visions of the hereafter. It doesn't occur, for instance, in most concepts of reincarnation, where the individual may suffer some sort of imperfect punishment in their successive lives, but the original sin or crime is never erased. In the vision of the afterlife offered here, however, we may now be able to erase and rewrite all such incidents and make perfect atonement and redemption possible. And, most importantly, in this atonement and redemption is the growth of the soul.

Dante, in the *Purgatorio*, borrows the Greek concept of the River Lethe —the river of forgetfulness—and adapts it to his own ends. As souls approach heaven, they may drink from Lethe, but rather than total forgetfulness of their past life, they forget only their sins. Dante also introduces a new river, Eunoe, which, if drank from, reinforces our memories of good deeds we've done. Although this is only a poetic myth, it expresses the natural desire, not just to atone for and repair harmful acts, but to virtually erase and replace them. The memory of evil, even if far in the past and properly atoned for, is still like a weight on our soul. The simple memory of it is like a residue which brings it back into existence, however reduced.

Dante's poetic concept is interesting. At some point, once we have learned any lesson to be learned for the growth of our soul, it appears that such memories serve no further purpose. Painful memories, whether of harm we've suffered or harm we've committed, oppress us and make it impossible for our soul ever to "fly." In this case, forgetfulness is blessed. But this should never take place until after such sins have been expiated in the way we've described.

Nietzsche talks about this a little in his book, *Untimely Meditations*: "Man braces himself against the great and ever greater pressure of what is past: it pushes him down or bends him sideways, it encumbers his steps as a dark, invisible burden . . . Forgetting is essential to action of any kind . . . A man who could forget nothing would be like one forcibly deprived of sleep, or an animal that had to live only by rumination and ever repeated rumination. Thus it is possible to live almost without memory (as animals do), but it is altogether impossible to live *well* without forgetting."[143] Once our misdeed is atoned for and forgiven, it may as well also be forgotten. This is all the more so if the harmful incident can be recreated or rewritten in a positive way.

It's a common belief in many cultures that we shouldn't speak ill of the dead, and, similarly, if we harbor resentments, we should let go of them and try to forgive. If the deceased should wish to make amends or atone for harm done in their past life, they won't be able to do so until the person harmed joins them in the afterlife. Until that becomes possible, their soul may feel disquieted. But if the individual still living has already forgiven them, the urgency of the need for atonement will be eased and their disquiet calmed. Later, when they are together in the hereafter, the atonement (and redemption) may be made perfect. This, incidentally, may also point to the value of prayer for the deceased, as some religions advocate, since such prayer is already an expression of goodwill and lack of resentment toward them.

I can imagine that a great deal of time might be spent in this sort of activity in the afterlife. This could come to include both sins of commission and sins of omission, or rather, all of the important things we had left undone. I've sometimes thought that if I were to be judged in the next world, it wouldn't be so much for all of the bad things I've done, which perhaps were not that many, but for all of the good things I didn't do. In the afterlife, I'd now have the opportunity to remedy this. This act of omission is actually one of the seven deadly vices, namely, "sloth." We generally think of sloth as meaning physical laziness, but the original meaning, from the Latin, "*acedia*," was closer to spiritual laziness, that is, a lack of zeal in pursuing the good. Dante, in *The Purgatorio*, assigns this vice to the fourth level of purgatory, and in Canto VII, refers to "not what I did but what I left undone."

And beyond this is the issue of missed opportunities. The poets tell us that the saddest thing in life is "What might have been," all of those numberless missed opportunities that might have added great value to our earthly narrative. This, I think, is what plagues us the most, this notion that we have only one life to live. How many of us have the wisdom to get it right the first time? What if we had only one chance to learn to ride a bike or to learn to swim? If we didn't get it right on the first try, that would be the end of it. A few might be able to do it, but most would not. Then what of something infinitely more complex like learning how to live well? Who hasn't thought at times that if they had the chance to do it all over again, they'd do it differently—to create a completely new "narrative"? Would you like to have tried another occupation or career? Perhaps several? Have there been missed opportunities in love? Perhaps you could relive your life with another person. Perhaps several different lives with different careers and different people. To take our life and relive it over and over but each time differently—even when the goal is not to make amends to others for harm done, but to make amends to ourselves for opportunities lost, to experience the endless variety and novelty life offers. If in the afterlife our dreams take the force of reality and other souls find it agreeable, such things might pleasurably fill an eternity.

It may occur to some that in the same way that immortality would be a problem in our earthly lives by contributing to crushing boredom, it would likewise become a problem in the afterlife.

But there is an important difference. Earlier we mentioned that no matter how much novelty we might introduce to our lives, we could never overcome the fact that we ourselves, our personalities and the way we perceive the world, inevitably becomes fixed and "stale." In the hereafter, though, this would no longer be the case, since each time we merged with another, we'd grow, we'd become a new person, we'd be "renewed." And our perception of the world would alter accordingly.

Wisdom is sometimes found in the unlikeliest places, and I'm reminded here of the film, Groundhog Day, with Bill Murray. Murray's character, a kind of self-centered oaf, is forced to live the same day over and over, essentially until he gets it right. At first, the extreme tedium of reliving the same day leads him to despair and attempted suicide. When he discovers it isn't possible to kill himself, it slowly occurs to him to see the situation as an opportunity. He devotes every minute of the day to good deeds, acts of kindness, and cultivating talents that we all wish we had taken the time to learn. He learns to play the piano as a way to give pleasure not just for himself but for others as well. He discovers that a single day, if lived rightly, can be a microcosm for an entire life. When he finally does these things he's freed from the endless repetition and is allowed to continue with his life now with new insight. It may be that it's precisely this sort of thing that is made possible in the afterlife.

In Part One we examined Ovid's saying that we cannot determine whether a person has had a happy life until the time of their death.

Presumably, Ovid's meaning was that a person's fortunes could change at any time and an otherwise happy life could end in great misfortune. For instance, some or all of an individual's life goals could be dashed and left unfulfilled. In the *Nicomachean Ethics*, Aristotle takes Ovid's saying a step further and asks: "Are the dead affected by the fortunes of those who survive them?"[144] In other words, he asks whether we cannot judge of someone's happiness even at the time of death, but must wait to see what transpires afterward. For instance, if their children suffer misfortune, wouldn't this undermine their happiness? He writes: "For it is popularly believed that some good and evil such as honors or dishonors, and successes and disasters of his children and descendants generally—can happen to a dead man, inasmuch as they can happen to a live one without his being aware of them."[145]

We're familiar with the idea that the living miss and grieve for loved ones who had passed on, but wouldn't the reverse also be true? Isn't it natural to believe that the deceased would also miss and grieve over their separation from loved ones left behind, even from their heavenly vantage point? It seems as if not to do so would be a betrayal of their love for those still in their earthly existence. And beyond simply missing them, wouldn't it also be expected that they would have great concern for the welfare of those they loved? Particularly, for example, their children and spouse? If this is true, it would mean that the hereafter is not always purely joyful—there may be some *angst* in heaven.

But is it necessary for there to be an afterlife for Aristotle's question to be answered positively? If there were no afterlife, could the fate of loved ones still matter to the deceased? Aristotle's statement that bad things could be considered to happen to a "dead man, inasmuch as they can happen to a live one without his being aware of them" implies that he is including the possibility that there is no afterlife. As strange as it sounds, even in this case an argument could be made that the happiness of the dead man could be affected—retroactively, by rendering it illusory and meaningless. For example, if the individual's happiness during life was centered around his progeny, his children and grandchildren and their prosperity, then if they suffered great misfortune such as financial destitution or premature death, this would appear to jeopardize the foundation of his happiness, that is, it would undermine what had been most meaningful to him.

It's true that if there is no afterlife the departed would not be aware of such misfortunes, yet if they had known as they approached the end of life that their children's lives would end tragically, and that they would have no descendents, they might judge their own life to have been pointless. Or if a person had worked all their life to build up a thriving business which they hoped to pass on to their son, but upon their death their son sold off everything and spent the proceeds on dissipation and debauchery, this would retroactively made a mockery of their lifelong project. That which made them most happy would prove to have been a delusion. It's similar, as Aristotle hints, to the case of an individual who places great value on his belief that he is admired and respected by all of his co-workers, while, in truth, they are mocking and laughing at him behind his back. He may not be aware of the truth, but if he were, he would realize that his happiness is based upon a falsehood. This seems to imply that, contrary to Ovid, even at the time of a man's death we cannot judge him to have had a meaningful life, since he may have been happy in his ignorance, but it's meaning would be undermined.

No doubt, if an individual sees their own life's narrative as incorporating the life narratives of their children, and perhaps even to future generations beyond that, then their happiness would be extraordinarily precarious. Even if we say there is no afterlife, it would retroactively put at impossible risk that which had given their life meaning.

In truth, we're trying to get at something more important here. The problem may be in Ovid's asking whether a man can be judged to have had a "happy" life until the time of his death. The solution, I think, is in choosing carefully what we devote our life to. We should choose goals or life activities which are good in themselves, whether their attainment is within our lifespan or extends beyond it. The pursuit of truth or goodness or beauty, for example, rather than reputation or material prosperity for ourselves and our descendents, are ends which are good in themselves and can constitute happiness even if not completely fulfilled in one's lifetime. This is true even if they are reversed after death, since we have no control over this, and we can say at least that we did all that we could do in the brief span of a lifetime. Aristotle tells us that, "we ought, so far as in us lies, to put on immortality, and do all that we can to live in conformity with the highest that is in us; for even if it is small in bulk, in power and preciousness, it far excels all the rest. Indeed it would seem that this is the true self of the individual, since it is the authoritative and better part of him."[146]

If our happiness depended upon the perpetual good fortune of all of our descendents, then it's certain to be disappointed, if not by our children, then perhaps by our great-great-grandchildren. Even if in "heaven" we happened to see calamity befall our children, from this vantage point we may be able to see it as the playing out of their destiny and a necessary part of their soul's education. And finally, life, after all, is short, which means that not only are life's joys brief, but so are its sorrows, and we would know that our loved ones would not be long in joining us.

Aristotle has his own take on it. He appears not be convinced of the soul's persistence in an afterlife, but in either case, one's happiness will not be greatly affected by the fortunes of those left behind. This is all the more so as his descendents are increasingly removed from him over the generations. Aristotle observes: "It is questionable whether the departed have any participation in good or its opposite . . . If any effect of good or evil reaches them at all, it must be faint or slight, either in itself or to them—or if not that, at any rate not of such force or quality . . . as to rob the happy of their felicity. So it appears the dead are affected to some extent by the good fortunes of those whom they love, and similarly by their misfortunes, but that the effects are not of such a kind or so great as to make the happy unhappy, or to produce any other such result."[147]

Chapter 8

A Sensible Afterlife

"I shall pass willingly to that eternal sleep, which, whether with, or without dreams, awaits us hereafter."[148]
—Thomas Jefferson

Thus far I've suggested five ways in which an especially harmful person in their earthly life might meet with justice in the afterlife:

1) In the afterlife, the deceased can now, after reviewing their life, see more clearly the wrong they've done and feel genuine remorse;
2) If they merge with people they've harmed, they will experience the harm they've done first-hand, now as the victim—this is perfect justice;
3) other souls may not wish to merge with them at all;
4) even if they are merged into a group-soul, they may not be permitted to participate in the group dream;
5) if they are permitted to participate in the group dream, it may be in a compensatory role to right the wrong they've committed and redeem themselves.

All along in our speculation we've proceeded on the assumption that, first, the universe is essentially good, it is benign and even joyful, as expressing the purpose of its Creator. And second, that the harmful individual will meet with justice, but will do so in a way that leads to greater self-knowledge and goodness. For these reasons, I would choose numbers one, two, and five as the most probable from our list. The last, allowing the harm-doer a compensatory role, seems especially fruitful to me, since in this way remorse may lead to redemption. Remorse is the most profound catalyst toward self-knowledge, and redemption is its attainment.

Remember that we are only trying to outline some possibilities for what the afterlife might be like. Truth, goodness, and beauty will have the most meaning in our earthly lives if they find expression most fully in the afterlife, with the former a kind of training for the latter.

In the afterlife we have a new power—our dreams or the projections of our imaginations take on a new level of reality.[149] And the more people we merge with, the more real is the dream. These are *waking dreams*, however, and are the products of our conscious minds. It makes sense that we would have this new power since it is appropriate that the afterlife somehow be a progression on our earthly life. The purpose of growth in self-knowledge is to be able to use this new power wisely in these waking dreams.

The German philosopher, Immanuel Kant, believed that the foundation for all morality was the creation of the "good will." In *Groundwork of a Metaphysics of Morals,* he writes: "It is impossible to conceive anything at all in the world, or even out of it, which can be taken as good without qualification, except a *good will*. Intelligence, wit, judgment, and any other talents of the mind we may care to name, or courage, resolution, and constancy of purpose, as qualities of temperament, are without doubt good and desirable in many respects; but they can also be extremely bad and hurtful when the will is not good."[150] In an afterlife in which our wishes or "wills" become reality, nothing could be more important or valuable than the creation of such good wills. From good wills come good intentions toward others. And such good intentions would give form to dreams of harmony and peace. When our wills give shape to reality, then, truly, rectitude derives not from what we do but what we intend—or rather, in this case, what we will and what we do are the same thing. It's difficult not to be reminded here of Jesus' teaching in the Sermon on the Mount that we must not only not do evil, but must also not think it.[151] Here, sin equals bad intent or the "bad will." Once more, the formation of the "good will" will come from self-knowledge—the self-knowledge we gain in our lifetime, plus the knowledge we gain in merging with others in the afterlife.

Earlier, I hinted that we would have "bodies" in the group dreams of the afterlife. Although these bodies would be our own projection, they would be real enough. We could still experience all the sights and sounds and tastes and smells of our former life, all of which would derive from a kind of extremely vivid "remembering." We could imagine ourselves to be hungry and it would be so. We could imagine eating food and satisfying our hunger. In doing so, we could experience and enjoy the taste of the food—again, based on a perfect recall of the taste of the food we had eaten in our lifetime. By this reasoning, I suppose, we would not be able to experience the taste of any food in the afterlife which we had not experienced in our earthly life. However, in merging with others and assuming their memories, we should be able to include memories of their experiences, the foods they had tasted, and so on. This shouldn't be so surprising a thought, since, even in our earthly lives, we sometimes dream of eating food, such as something sweet, like chocolate, or sour, like a lemon, and experience the taste vividly in the dream although it is only imagined. We're able to do this through an extremely lucid remembering of times when we had actually tasted these foods. Likewise, we know that when a person is hypnotized, they can be made to grimace and pucker their mouth if told they're eating a lemon, although no object is present. If these sort of reflections sound odd, it's worth noting that even the Bible speaks of "angels' food."[152] And Milton, in Book V of <u>Paradise Lost</u>, writes of the angels:

> Forthwith from dance to sweet repast they turn
> Desirous; all in circles as they stood,
> Tables are set, and on a sudden piled
> With Angels' food, and rubied nectar flows:
> In pearl, in diamond and massy gold,
> Fruit of delicious vines, the growth of Heaven.
> On flowers reposed, and with fresh flowerlets crowned,
> They eat, they drink, and in communion sweet
> Quaff immortality and joy . . . [153]

We shouldn't exclude the possibility, then, that in the afterlife, through the same means of a more perfect recall, we can experience all of the normal sensations of our earthly lives. And the greater the number of souls in the group-soul, the more this will be so.

I suppose we might ask ourselves whether we could imagine experiencing sexual desire just as we had imagined hunger for food? Possibly, but if we simply imagined ourselves having a partner to express this desire, our experience would be no more real than the fantasies we had in our earthly lives. Our partner would be strictly imaginary. But if we merged our soul with another, who willingly joined in the "dream," it would take on a new level of reality. And, in fact, with the merging of souls, such a "sexual" dream could be filled with true intimacy and love. Having said all of this, it may be far more likely that the merging or melting together of souls would already be so joyous that the recreation of a sexual dream would be pointless. If we had previously scanned the life of the other person and experienced it completely through their eyes, and all of their senses, then it could probably be said that we had already possessed that person's body wholly.

My only intention here is to suggest that in any "sensible" afterlife, it seems necessary that we are still in some possession of our senses. Are we to be deaf, dumb, and blind in the hereafter? People sometimes speak of a celestial music or the heavenly "music of the spheres." Milton in *Paradise Lost* writes of the ambrosial fragrances that filled all heaven."[154]* We often hear of a "beatific vision." Why not a beatific felicity for all the senses, not just the eyes?

The early Christian philosopher, Augustine of Hippo (St. Augustine) 354-430 AD, believed that the soul, when it leaves the body, takes all of its powers with it. "The soul withdraws from the body taking all with itself, sense and imagination, reason, understanding and intelligence, the concupiscible and irascible powers."[155]

Amazingly, C.S. Lewis takes up the theme of sexuality in heaven in his book, *Miracles*. He introduces the subject rather coyly: "One point must be touched on because, though I kept silence, it would none the less be present in most reader's minds." He goes on to say: "We know the sexual life; we do not know, except in glimpses, the other thing, which, in Heaven, will leave no room for it. Hence, where fullness awaits us, we anticipate fasting. In denying that sexual life, as we now understand it, makes any part of the final beatitude, it is not of course necessary to suppose that the distinction of sexes will disappear. What is no longer

---

* In *Paradise Lost*, Milton's description of Eden, the earthly paradise, can be taken for his portrayal of heaven, since in Christian thought and in Milton's own words, Eden is regarded as heaven on earth. In Book IV he writes: "A Heaven on Earth: for blissful Paradise of God the garden was, by Him in the east of Eden planted." He describes Eden according to his poetic fancy, which I've put in Appendix B for anyone who might be interested.

needed for biological purposes may be expected to survive for splendor . . . Neither men nor women will be asked to throw away weapons they have used victoriously. It is the beaten and the fugitives who throw away their swords. The conquerors sheathe and retain them . . . 'Trans-sexual' would be a better word than 'sexless' for the heavenly life."[156]

Lewis, perhaps, needs to "sheathe" his own sword and cool off a little. It's not completely clear what he means when he suggests that in heaven we'll all be "trans-sexual" but presumably he uses the prefix "trans" to mean "beyond" rather than "across." On the other hand, I suppose that if in the merging process we become in effect, "two-in-one," and incorporate all of the life memories of the other, then the merging of souls of a man and a woman would result in a kind of "transexual" being.

Although it's enjoyable to poke fun at C.S. Lewis, he nevertheless has a worthwhile point to make. He continues with some embarrassment, "I am well aware that this last paragraph may seem to many readers unfortunate and to some comic. But that very comedy is the symptom of our estrangement, as spirits, from Nature and our estrangement, as animals, from Spirit."[157]

Along this line, the one time in which Jesus of Nazareth gives a specific answer regarding the nature of heaven is when the Sadducees ask him about the teaching of Moses that, "If a man dies, having no children, his brother as next of kin shall marry his wife, and raise up an offspring to his brother." Hoping to baffle Jesus, the Sadducees concocted the following strange question: "Now there were seven brothers with us; and the first married and died, and having no offspring left his wife to his brother; so also the second, and third, down to the seventh. And last of all, the woman died. In heaven therefore whose wife of the seven shall she be? For they all had her." To this Jesus responded: "You are mistaken, not understanding the Scriptures, or the power of God. For in Heaven they neither marry, nor are given in marriage, but are like angels in heaven."[158] This is a good answer. Of course our wedding vows are only made "til death do us part." Presumably, after that time, our nuptial obligations come to an end. I suspect though that the dearest wish of many couples who had spent long and loving lives together is to stay together always.[.]

[.] It might have been better if the seven Sadducee brothers had spent more time trying to figure out why every brother who married this woman died. Was it her cooking? Was she a black-widow murderess? Apparently, she was

Although the union of two or more souls could not of course produce a child or "offspring," they might perhaps "adopt" or become the caretaker for a child or infant who had died during infancy or childbirth. The group soul could serve as a kind of extended family for it. In many ways, this is a comforting thought. It doesn't seem appropriate for this infant-soul to immediately merge with others, since at this point it would not yet have developed any separate identity of its own. It might be allowed to interact with other "infant-souls" like itself. The process could be gradual.

There is another sense in which the union of two souls could be said to produce an offspring. The soul created by their merging could be regarded as a new soul, a synthesis of the two. In our earthly lives, when two individuals have a child, the child is a new combination of the genes contributed by both parents. In the afterlife the new composite-soul is a combination of the life memories of the two souls. But the process, you might say, is reversed. On earth the process is from the one to the many. In the afterlife it is from the many to the one, as souls are, so to speak, gathered back into the fold.

The new power acquired in the afterlife requires a new level of responsibility and self-understanding. We may or may not have attained such understanding in our former life. Perhaps many do not. The *Tibetan Book of the Dead* (a Buddhist tract) declares that the individual who has recently died may begin to project nightmarish dreams if they had not attained enlightenment during their lifetime. The book does not say that there are other souls that can be merged with, but that the isolated individual should move toward and merge with a divine light which will lead them to the state of *nirvana*, and the extinguishing of self. The word "*nirvana*" means "to blow out" as in the snuffing of a candle. "Self" for the Buddhists represents separation and therefore suffering.

I would like to suggest that the goal should not be the extinguishing of self but the augmentation of self. I do not really believe that the newly deceased is likely to be engulfed in nightmares. First of all, they will possess a tremendous new clarity of thought, and will be functioning from their conscious mind, not their subconscious. Even in our earthly lives we

---

the one dispatching them and sending them off to heaven. After the first two or three brothers died, what brother would have the courage to be the next in line? Jesus should have talked about this a little. It could have made a good parable supporting abstinence or the virtues of bachelorhood.

only experience nightmares when we're asleep and our conscious mind is more or less turned off. Second, if we do feel uneasy in some way at our newfound abilities, other souls will be available to guide us or merge with us to increase our understanding. Comfort will be immediately available. The authors of the *Tibetan Book of the Dead* state that we may see other deceased souls around us but it will not be possible to communicate with them. It's my own feeling that growth in knowledge and wisdom requires that we be able to communicate with other souls in the most intimate way—that is, by merging. In any case, if I were to guess, I'd say that perhaps the beautiful white light that the Buddhists speak of is actually the "all-soul," the composite soul of all those who had lived and died and merged together in an eternity of time. Moving toward this light, however, would not involve the snuffing out of our individual soul, but rather its infinite augmentation and expansion as we came to participate in the extraordinarily beatific dream of the "All-Soul."

Occasionally, Nietzsche, in his philosophical reveries, hits on images reminiscent of such a universal soul: "Anyone who managed to experience the history of humanity as a whole *as his own history* will feel in an enormously generalized way all the grief of an invalid who thinks of health, of an old man who thinks of the dreams of his youth, of a lover deprived of his beloved, of the martyr whose ideal is perishing, of the hero on the evening after the battle that decided nothing but brought him wounds and the loss of his friend. But if one endured, if one *could* endure this immense sum of grief of all kinds while yet being the hero, who, as the second day of battle breaks, welcomes the dawn and his fortune, being a person whose horizon encompasses thousands of years past and future, being the heir of all the nobility of all past spirit; . . . If one could burden one's soul with all of this—the oldest, the newest, losses, hopes, conquests, and the victories of humanity, if one could finally contain all this in one soul and crowd it into a single feeling—this would surely have to result in a happiness that humanity has not known so far; the happiness of a god full of power and love, full of tears and laughter, a happiness that, like the sun in the evening, continually bestows its inexhaustible riches, pouring them into the sea, feeling richest, as the sun does, when even the poorest fisherman is still rowing with golden oars!"[159] But Nietzsche here is only describing the merging of a kind of universal collective soul and not the next phase, the collective dream, wherein finally, "this immense sum of grief," is lifted from our backs and replaced by a brilliant clarity, a gentle grace, and luminous beauty.

In the *Nicomachean Ethics*, Aristotle poses the question as to what sort of activity would occupy the gods. He is doubtful whether many of the activities and values meaningful to humans—justice, courage, liberality, moderation (the cardinal virtues)—would have any relevance for gods. "The gods in our conception of them are supremely happy and blessed but what kind of actions should be attributable to them? If we say 'Just actions,' surely we shall be confronted by the absurdity of their making contracts and returning deposits and all that sort of thing. Shall we say 'brave actions'—facing terrors and risking their persons in the cause of honor? What of liberal actions? They will have nobody to give to; . . . What form could their temperate actions take? Surely it would be cheap praise, since they have no evil desires!"[160] Aristotle glosses over the fact that as soon as we refer to "gods" in the plural, the argument can be made that they are not gods at all, at least in the modern conception that a "god" must be omnipotent and omniscient. If there is more than one god then their power must be limited accordingly. And if their power is limited, then they cannot be completely self-sufficient, they must have needs. They are simply more powerful beings, but not gods.

The Greek poet, Homer, in the *Odyssey* and *The Iliad*, presents a pantheon of gods coexisting on Mount Olympus. They are very human-like, very needy, and often at odds with on another. They are, however, immortal. One contemporary philosopher, Martha Nussbaum, suggests that because of their immortality, their attitude toward their lives is rather playful. No great harm, including pain and death, can come to them. Everything, even their warring with one another, is done with a light touch. Nussbaum, like Aristotle, argues that this invulnerability and immortality negates the possibility for virtuous action of any kind, and, in fact, "would bring about the death of value as we know it."[161] She argues that courage is no longer relevant since "courage consists in a certain way of acting and reacting in the face of death and the risk of it. A being who cannot take that risk cannot have that virtue."[162] But I think that there are other kinds of courage other than just displays of physical courage. For instance, in our vision of heaven here, each individual soul would show considerable courage in merging with anyone they'd formerly harmed. It could not be pleasant to see ourselves in this light. Courage would also be displayed by the former "victim" willing to merge with the person who had harmed them.

Nussbaum, like Aristotle, sees no opportunity for justice, again, since she feels that this has to do primarily with the distribution of goods, which will no longer apply in a world without bodily needs. But of course one beautiful aspect of the "merging" of souls, as we've described it, is that it provides for perfect justice, along with the real possibility of forgiveness and continued growth of the soul. Even the virtue of moderation continues to be important since heaven must be shared with so many other souls. Nussbaum states that friendship and love will also no longer have meaning, since, as she says, this cannot be expressed in the form of giving one's life to another. Here again, though, the result of the merging of two souls and the complete scanning of each other's life would likely create the kind of bond formed in a long, loving marriage or lifetime friendship. In this context, Aristotle's "liberality" becomes especially fitting as individual souls seek to give pleasure to others in the ways we've already described. One could even assert, in a manner of speaking, that each soul upon merging takes on the sins and the pain of the other. Each soul imparts wisdom to the other, not just in sharing all of the good things in its life, but also all of its difficulties and trials.

In the thought-experiment conducted here, souls in the afterlife are immortal, and, to that extent, god-like, but ultimately for the reasons already given, they are not gods. The extent of their life may be unlimited but their power is not. They must share heaven with all the other multitude of souls. It may also be important to realize that they have made the transition from mortality (or the presumption of mortality) to immortality. This god-like quality is new to them. They arrive in the afterlife from a state of human finitude and weakness. That the exercise of most of the virtues is still possible is clear.

We began by asking what sort of afterlife would most make sense of our earthly life. Our answer is that it would have to be one which incorporated both justice for those who had done wrong, and yet be merciful and forgiving to allow for a continued growth of the soul. This would be accomplished by the merging of souls. Justice would be achieved in ways that we've already described, but particularly, if we should merge with someone we had harmed, we'd then experience our wrongdoing as its victim. This would be perfect justice, and yet make possible the growth of self-knowledge at the same time. In fact, the symmetry involved in the mutual scanning process makes possible not only perfect justice but perfect forgiveness, and perfect atonement and redemption.

The afterlife would have to be, in some way, both serious and playful, to combine the ethical and the aesthetic. We can combine the two in the concept of the collective dream of a group-soul. The individual member of the group-soul would need to have grown in wisdom and moral sense to make the fullest contribution to the collective dream. Such a dream would not be frivolous, but guided by truth, goodness and beauty. In turn, the creativity expressed in this contribution is the highest form of the aesthetic expressed as play. This sort of resolution of the tension between philosophical concepts as justice and mercy, justice and the growth of the soul, between the ethical and the aesthetic (morality and play), argue in favor of this model of the afterlife.

At this highest level, the concepts of truth and goodness and beauty begin to merge—they all become translatable into one another. In our existence on earth we find that goodness is based on our level of self-knowledge, but that this self-knowledge rarely becomes complete in the span of a single lifetime. In the hereafter we have the opportunity to increase this knowledge by merging with others and thereby also perfect our goodness. Likewise, as the possibility of doing harm to others in the afterlife is greatly diminished, goodness is expressed primarily in the form of giving pleasure, putting it into the realm of the aesthetic, that is, of beauty and play.

If I can employ a loose analogy, physicists tell us that the four fundamental forces of nature all merge into one force when under extreme temperatures like those present during the Big Bang or conception of the universe. In a similar way, truth and goodness and beauty, and indeed, all of the virtues begin to merge in the afterlife. That all of the virtues are one was one of the central teachings of Plato and Socrates, but it may be that this only finds the fullest expression in the hereafter.

I believe the vision of "heaven" offered here infuses meaning into our earthly lives. Given such a vision, how would we choose to live? What are the implications for the conduct of our lives? It seems to me that we would use our lives to cultivate our own unique individuality and potential to the fullest. We ought to be dissuaded from harming others since to do harm would only mean we'd need to expiate our misdeeds in the ways described above. And, it should not be forgotten, every generous and kind action we'd performed in life would give us great pleasure in the hereafter when we now were on the receiving end.

Life and death, in this conception, become two halves of a perfect whole, expressing both coherence and harmony, two of the elements of beauty. This is in contrast to other portraits of the afterlife, such as the Christian Heaven/Hell or Buddhist concept of reincarnation, which seem to lack any logical or necessary connection between life and afterlife. Beyond the perfect symmetry already discussed, this solution displays tremendous economy in using a minimum number of assumptions to explain an array of variables, such as justice, truth, goodness, beauty, atonement, and so forth. And finally, this economy gives form to a kind of grace or elegance of expression in the sense that it flows freely and naturally from a few simple assumptions. All of these qualities are attributes of beauty and regarded by philosophers and scientists as favorable indicators that they're traveling on the right path.

Why is this a "philosopher's view of heaven?" Because it begins with the pursuit of truth and self-knowledge, both in this life and the next, which, in turn, becomes the foundation for the creation of an afterlife suffused with goodness and beauty. Finally, such an afterlife would justify and make sense of our earthly lives in the fullest possible way.

Rene Descartes believed that if we can imagine perfection, its very perfection is an argument in favor of its existence. Perfection is self-justifying, it is its own rationale. Perfection, we might say, *deserves* to exist. If we were gods, and we could imagine a perfect world, we would bring it into being. In this essay, I've tried to describe a perfect afterlife, and one which when combined with our earthly life, forms a perfect coherent whole. At this point, we've perhaps taken our thought-experiment as far as it can be taken and should bring it to an end. However, we might at least say with Socrates that "either this or something very like it is a true account of our souls and their future habitation."[163]

APPENDIX A

References to Heaven in the Koran

And give glad tidings unto those who believe and do good works; that theirs are Gardens underneath which rivers flow; as often as they are regaled with food of the fruit thereof; (II, 25)

For those who keep from evil, with their Lord, are Gardens underneath which rivers flow, and pure companions, and contentment from Allah. (III, 15)

There doth every soul experience that which it did aforetime. (X, 31)

A similitude of the Garden which is promised unto those who keep their duty to Allah: Underneath it rivers flow; its food is everlasting, and its shade; this is the reward of those who keep their duty, while the reward of disbelievers is the Fire. (XIII, 35)

Lo! Those who ward off evil are among gardens and water springs. And it is said unto them, Enter them in peace, secure. And we remove whatever rancor may be in their breasts. As brethren, face to face, they rest on couches raised. Toil cometh not unto them there, nor will they be expelled from thence. (XV, 45-48)

Gardens of Eden which they enter, underneath which rivers flow, wherein they have what they will. Thu Allah repayeth those who ward off evil. (XVI, 31)

As for such, theirs will be Gardens of Eden, wherein rivers flow beneath them; therein they will be given armlets of gold and will wear green robes of finest silk and gold embroidery, reclining on thrones therein. Blest the reward, and fair the resting-place! (XVIII, 32)

Lo! Those who believe and do good works, theirs are the Gardens of Paradise for welcome, wherein they will abide, with no desire to be removed from thence. (XIX, 108-109)

They hear therein no idle talk, but only Peace; and therein they have food for morn and evening. (XIX, 62)

Gardens of Eden! They enter them wearing armlets of gold and pearl and their raiment therein is silk. And they say, Praise be to Allah who hath put grief away from us. Lo! Our Lord is Forgiving, Bountiful. Who, of his Grace, hath installed us in the mansion of eternity, where toil toucheth us not nor can weariness affect us. (XXXV, 33-35)

For them there is known provision, Fruits. And they will be honored in the Gardens of delight, on couches facing one another; A cup from a gushing spring is brought round for them, White, delicious to the drinkers, Wherein there is no headache nor are they made mad thereby. And with them are those of modest gaze, with lovely eyes, Pure as they were hidden eggs of the ostrich. (XXXVII, 41-49)

Gardens of Eden, whereof the gates are opened for them, Wherein, reclining, they call for plenteous fruit and cool drink that is therein. And with them are those of modest gaze, companions. (XXXVIII, 51-53)

But those who keep their duty to their Lord, for them are lofty halls with lofty halls above them, built for them, beneath which rivers flow. It is a promise of Allah. Allah faileth not His promise. (XXXIX, 20)

Oh my people! Lo! this life of the world is but a passing comfort, and lo! the Hereafter, that is the enduring home. (XL, 39)

Lo! those who say: Our Lord is Allah, and afterward are upright, the angels descend upon them, saying: Fear not nor grieve, but hear good tidings of the paradise which ye are promised. We are your protecting friends in the life of the world and in the Hereafter. There ye will have all that your souls desire, and there ye will have all for which ye pray. (XLI, 30-31)

Thou seest the wrong-doers fearful of that which they have earned, and it will surely befall them; while those who believe and do good works, will be in flowering meadows of the Gardens, having what they wish from their Lord. (XLII, 22)

Enter the Garden, ye and your wives, to be made glad. Therein are brought round for them trays of gold and goblets, and therein is all that souls desire and eyes find sweet. And ye are immortal therein. This is the Garden which ye are made to inherit because of what ye used to do. (XLIII, 70-72)

Lo! those who kept their duty will be in a place secure amid gardens and water-springs, attired in silk and silk-embroidery, facing one another. Even so it will be. And we shall wed them unto fair ones with wide, lovely eyes. They call therein for every fruit in safety. They taste not death therein, save the first death. (XLIV, 51-56)

Therein are rivers of water unpolluted, and rivers of milk whereof the flavor changeth not, and rivers of wine delicious to the drinkers, and rivers of clear-run honey; therein for them is every kind of fruit, with pardon from their Lord. (XLVII, 15)

Lo! Those who kept their duty dwell in gardens and delight. Happy because of what their Lord hath given them. And it is said unto them: Eat and drink in health as reward for what ye used to do. Reclining on ranged couches. And we wed them unto fair ones with wide, lovely eyes. And they who believe and whose seed follow them in faith, We cause their seed to join them, and we deprive them of naught of their life's work. Every man is a pledge for that which he hath earned. And we provide them with fruit and meat such as they desire. (LII, 17-22)

For them who feareth the standing before the Lord there are two gardens. Of spreading branches. Wherein are two fountains flowing. Wherein is every kind of fruit in pairs. Reclining upon couches lined with silk brocade, the fruit of both gardens near to hand. Therein are those of modest gaze, who neither man nor jinni will have touched before them. In beauty like the jacinth and the coral-stone. Is the reward of goodness aught but goodness? And beside them are two other gardens. Dark green with foliage. Wherein are two abundant springs. Wherein is fruit, the date-palm and pomegranate. Wherein are found the good and beautiful fair ones, close-guarded in pavilions whom neither man nor jinni will have touched before them. Reclining on green cushions and fair carpets. (LV, 46-76)

And the foremost in the race, those are they who will be brought nigh in gardens of delight. A multitude of those of old and a few of those of later time, on lined couches, reclining therein face to face. There wait on them immortal youths, with bowls and ewers and a cup from a pure spring, wherefrom they get no aching of the head nor any madness. And fruit that they prefer. And flesh of fowls that they desire. And there are fair ones with wide, lovely eyes. Like unto hidden pearls. Reward for what they used to do. Therein they hear no vain speaking or recrimination. Naught but the saying: Peace, and again Peace. And those on the right hand, what of those on the right hand? (for the women) Among thornless lote-trees and clustered plantains, and spreading shade, and water gushing, and fruit in plenty, neither out of reach nor yet forbidden, and raised couches; Lo! We have created them a new creation, and made them virgins, lovers, friends. (LVI, 10-37)

(Allah) hath awarded them for all that they endured, a Garden and silk attire; Reclining therein upon couches, they will find there neither heat of a sun nor bitter cold. The shade thereof is close upon them and the clustered fruits thereof bow down. Goblets of silver are brought round for them, and beakers as of glass. Bright as glass but made of silver, which they themselves have measured to the measure of their deeds. There are they watered with a cup whereof the mixture is of Zanjabil. The water of a spring therein, named Salsabil. There serve them youths of everlasting youth, whom, when thou seest, thou wouldst take for scattered pearls. When thou seest, thou wilt see there bliss and high estate. Their raiment will be fine green silk and gold embroidery. Bracelets of silver will they wear. Their Lord will slake their thirst with a pure drink. And it will be said unto them: Lo! This is a reward for you. Your endeavor upon earth hath found acceptance. (LXXVI, 11-22)

Lo! Those who kept their duty are amid shade and fountains. And fruits such as they desire. Unto them it is said: Eat, drink and welcome, O ye blessed, in return for what ye did. Thus do we reward the good. (LXXVII, 41-44)

APPENDIX B

Following is John Milton's description of paradise or "heaven on earth" from Book IV of *Paradise Lost*.

So on he fares, and to the border comes
Of Eden, where delicious Paradise,
Now nearer, crowns with her enclosure green,
As with a rural mound, the champaign head
Of a steep wilderness, whose hairy sides
With thickest overgrown, grotesque and wild,
Access denied, and overhead upgrew
Insuperable height of loftiest shade,
Cedar, and pine, and fir, and branching palm,
A sylvan scene, and, as the ranks ascend
Shade above shade, a woody theater
Of stateliest view. Yet higher than their tops
The verdurous wall of Paradise upsprung,
And higher than that wall a circling row
Blossoms and fruit at once of golden hue,
Appeared, with gay enamelled colours mixed,
On which the sun more glad impressed his beams
Than in fair evening cloud, or humid bow,
When God hath showered the earth: so lovely seemed
That landscape; and of pure, now purer air
Meets his approach, and to the heart inspires
Vernal delight and joy, able to drive
All sadness but despair. Now gentle gales,
Fanning their odoriferous wings, dispense
Native perfumes, and whisper whence they stole
Those balmy spoils. As when to them who sail
Beyond the Cape of Hope, and now are part
Mozambic, off at sea north-east winds blow

Sabean odors from the spicy shore
Of Araby, the Blest, with such delay
Well pleased they slack their course, and many a league
Cheered with the grateful smell old Ocean smiles;

. . . . .

In narrow room Nature's whole wealth, yea more
A Heaven on Earth: for blissful Paradise
Of God the garden was, by him in the east
Of Eden planted; Eden stretched her line
From Auren eastward to the royal towers
Of great Seleucia, built by Grecian kings,
Or where the sons of Eden long before
Dwelt in Telassar. In this pleasant soil
His far more pleasant garden God ordained.
Out of the fertile ground he caused to grow
All trees of noblest kind for sight, smell, taste;
And all amid them stood the Tree of Life,
High eminent, blooming ambrosial fruit
Of vegetable gold, . . .
Southward through Eden went a river large,
Nor changed his course, but through the shaggy hill
Passed underneath engulfed, for God had thrown
That mountain, as his garden-mould, high raised
Upon the rapid current, which through veins
Of porous earth with kindly thirst up drawn
Rose a fresh fountain, and with many a rill
Watered the garden, thence united fell
Down the steep glade, . . .
But rather to tell how, if Art could tell
How, from the sapphire fount the crisped brooks,
Rolling on orient pearl and sands of gold,
With mazy error under pendant shades
Ran nectar, visiting each plant, and fed
Flowers worthy of Paradise, which not nice Art
In beds and curious knots, But Nature boon
Poured forth profuse on hill, and dale, and plain,

Both where the morning sun first warmly smote
The open field, and where the unpierced shade
Embrowned the noontide bowers. Thus was this place,
A happy rural seat of various view:
Groves whose rich trees wept odorous gums and balm;
Others whose fruit, burnished with golden rind,
Hung amiable, Hesperian fables true,
If true, here only, and of delicious taste;
Betwixt them lawns, or level downs, and flocks
Grazing the tender herb, were interposed,
Or palmy hillock or the flowery lap
Of some irriguous valley spread her store,
Flowers of all hue, and without thorn the rose.
Another side, umbrageous grots and caves
Of cool recess, o'er which the mantling vine
Lays forth her purple grape and gently creeps
Luxuriant; meanwhile murmuring water fall
Down the slope hills, dispersed, or in a lake,
That to the fringed bank with myrtle crowned
Her crystal mirror holds, unite their streams.
The birds their color apply; airs, vernal airs,
Breathing the smell of field and grove, attune
The trembling leaves, while universal Pan,
Knit with the Graces and the Hours in dance,
Led on the eternal Spring.

-Book IV, 131-268

REFERENCES

INTRODUCTION

1. Plato, *Apology*, in Edith Hamilton and Huntington Cairns, eds., *Plato: The Collected Dialogues*. Princeton University Press, Princeton, New Jersey, 1961, 40d, p. 25.
2. Twain, Mark, "The Damned Human Race," in *Letters from the Earth*, Fawcett Publications, Conn., 1968, p. 184.

PART ONE
MONTAIGNE ON THE FEAR OF DEATH

CHAPTER 1. KNOW YOUR ADVERSARY

3. Montaigne, Michel de, "That to philosophize is to learn to die," *The Complete Essays of Montaigne*, trans., Donald Frame, Stanford University Press, Stanford, Calif., 1965, I, 20, p. 60.
4. Ibid., p. 58.
5. Carlin, George, *An Orgy of George*, Hyperion, New York, 1997, pp. 837-838.
6. Montaigne, Michel de, "That the taste of good and evil depends in large part on the opinions we have of them," *The Complete Essays of Montaigne*, I, 14, p. 36.
7. Montaigne, Michel de, "That to philosophize is to learn to die," *The Complete Essays of Montaigne*, I, 20, p. 60.
8. Aurelius, Marcus, *Meditations*, Penguin Books, New York, 1985, Book Two, 12, p. 49.
9. Cicero, Marcus Tullius, *Cicero: Tusculan Disputations*, in Loeb Classical Library, Harvard University Press, Cambridge, Mass., 2001, III, xiv., 30, p. 295.

10.   Montaigne, Michel de, "Of the resemblance of children to fathers," *The Complete Essays of Montaigne*, II, 37, p. 576.

11.   Montaigne, Michel de, "Of vanity," *The Complete Essays of Montaigne*, III, 9, p. 753.

12.   Ibid.

13.   Montaigne, Michel de, "Of physiognomy," *The Complete Essays of Montaigne*, III, 12, p. 803.

14.   Ibid.

15.   Ibid., p. 804.

16.   Montaigne, Michel de, "Of practice," *The Complete Essays of Montaigne*, II, 6, p. 272.

17.   Ibid.

18.   Mencken, H.L., *A Mencken Chrestomathy*, Vintage Books, New York, 1949, p. 139.

19.   Montaigne, Michel de, "Of judging of the death of others," *The Complete Essays of Montaigne*, II, 13, p. 460.

CHAPTER 2. NATURE'S WAY

20.   Montaigne, Michel de, "That to philosophize is to learn to die," *The Complete Essays of Montaigne*, I, 20, p. 63.

21.   Emerson, Ralph Waldo, quoted in David Shields, *The Thing about Life is that One Day You'll be Dead*, Alfred A. Knopf, New York, 2008, p. 142.

22.   Montaigne, Michel de, "That to philosophize is to learn to die," *The Complete Essays of Montaigne*, I, 20, p. 63.

23.   Plato, *Republic*, in Edith Hamilton and Huntington Cairns, eds., *Plato: The Collected Dialogues*, Princeton University Press, Princeton, New Jersey, 1961, 329c.

24.   Seneca, Lucius Annaeus, "Letter 12: Old Age," *The Stoic Philosophy of Seneca, Essays and Letters*, W.W. Norton, New York, p. 176.

25.   Cicero, Marcus Tullius, "On Old Age," in *Cicero: Selected Works*, p. 232.

26.   Ibid., p. 293.

27.   Ibid., p. 241.

28.   Milton, John, *Paradise Lost*, Book XI, 535-538, p. 314, New American Library, New York, 1961.

29.   Montaigne, Michel de, "That to philosophize is to learn to die," *The Complete Essays of Montaigne*, I, 20, p. 67.

30. Rousseau, Jean-Jacques, *Emile*, trans., Allan Bloom, Basic Books, Inc., New York, 1979, Book II, p. 82.

31. Montaigne, Michel de, "That to philosophize is to learn to die," *The Complete Essays of Montaigne*, I, 20, p. 66.

32. Ibid.

33. Ibid., p. 65.

34. Ecclesiastes, The Old Testament, ii, 16.

35. Plato, *Apology*, in *Plato: The Collected Dialogues*, 29.

36. Ibid., *Apology*, 39d-41b.

37. Plato, *Phaedo*, 118, in *The Last Days of Socrates*, Penguin Classics, Baltimore, Maryland, 1969, p. 183.

38. Sophocles, *Oedipus at Colonus*, in *The Complete Plays of Sophocles*, Bantam Books, New York, p. 250.

39. Shakespeare, William, *Hamlet*, in W.G. Clark and W. Aldis Wright, eds., *The Complete Works of William Shakespeare,*, Nelson Doubleday, Inc., Garden City, New York, Act III, Scene I, 60-70.

40. Mencken, H.L., *A Mencken Chrestomathy*, p. 66.

41. Montaigne, Michel de, "Of practice," *The Complete Essays of Montaigne*, II, 6, p. 268.

42. Aurelius, Marcus, *Meditations*, Book Two, II, p. 48.

43. Mencken, H.L., *A Mencken Chrestomathy*, p. 131.

44. Plato, *Republic*, in *Plato: The Collected Dialogues*, 486, p. 722.

45. Aurelius, Marcus, *Meditations*, Book Four, 32, 33, pp. 70-71.

46. Ibid., *Meditations*, Book Ten, 17, p. 157.

47. Shakespeare, William, *As You Like It*, Act II, Scene 7, 139-143.

48. Pascal, Blaise, *Pensees* and Other Writings, trans., Honor Levi, Oxford University Press, 2008, IV, 102, p. 26.

49. Montaigne, Michel de, "Of vanity," *The Complete Essays of Montaigne*, III, 9, p. 752.

50. Ibid.

51. Mencken, H.L., *A Mencken Chrestomathy*, p. 138.

CHAPTER 3. OUR LEGACY

52. Seneca, Lucius Annaeus, "To Marcia on Consolation," *Seneca: Moral Essays*, in Loeb Classical Library, Harvard University Press, Cambridge, Mass., 1996, Vol. II, xxiii, 2, p. 83.

53. Cicero, Marcus Tullius, *Cicero: Tusculan Disputations*, in Loeb Classical Library, Harvard University Press, Cambridge, Mass., I, 86-87, p. 103.

54. Seneca, Lucius Annaeus, "To Marcia on Consolation," *Seneca: Moral Essays*, II, xx, 5, pp. 72-73.

55. Montaigne, Michel de, "All things have their season," *The Complete Essays of Montaigne*, II, 29, p. 531.

56. Ibid.

57. Cicero, Marcus Tullius, "On Old Age," in *Cicero: Selected Works*, Penguin Books, New York, 1971, p. 246.

58. Plutarch, "Whether an Old Man Should Engage in Public Affairs," in *Plutarch: Moralia*, Loeb Classical Library, Harvard University Press, Cambridge, Mass., 2002, Vol. X, 788, p. 105.

59. Montaigne, Michel de, "Of vanity," *The Complete Essays of Montaigne*, III, 9, pp. 724, 727.

60. Shaw, George Bernard, quoted in Susan K. Hom, *R.I.P.: The Famous Last Words, Epitaphs, Morbid Musings, and Fond Farewells of the Famous and Not-so-Famous*, Sterling, New York, 2007, p. 100.

61. Cicero, Marcus Tullius, "On Old Age," *Cicero: Selected Works*, p. 227.

62. Anonymous, quoted in Susan K. Hom, *R.I.P.: The Famous Last Words, Epitaphs, Morbid Musings, and Fond Farewells of the Famous and Not-so-Famous*, p. 26.

63. www.alsirat.com/epitaphs

64. Ibid.

65. Ibid.

66. Ibid.

67. Ibid.

68. Cicero, Marcus Tullius, *Cicero: Tusculan Disputations*, in Loeb Classical Library, Harvard University Press, Cambridge, Mass., VL, 95, p. 113.

69. Lucretius, *The Nature of Things*, trans., Frank Copley, W.W. Norton and Company, New York, Book III, 919-922, p. 77.

70. Ibid., Book III, 978-1012, p. 79.

71. Montaigne, Michel de, "That to philosophize is to learn to die," *The Complete Essays of Montaigne*, I, 20, p. 65.

72. Montaigne, Michel de, "That our happiness must not be judged until after our death," *The Complete Essays of Montaigne*, I, 19, p. 55.

73. Aristotle, *Nicomachean Ethics*, Penguin Books, New York, 1982, 1100a34-b26, p. 83.

74. Epictetus, *Discourses*, in Loeb Classical Library, Harvard University Press, Cambridge, Mass., 1985, IV, x, 10-15.

CHAPTER 4. SOCRATES' SECOND ALTERNATIVE

75. Montaigne, Michel de, "Of a Custom of Cea," *The Complete Essays of Montaigne*, II, 3, p. 254.

76. Burke, Edmund, *A Philosophical Enquiry into the Origin of Our Ideas of the Sublime and the Beautiful*, Oxford University Press, Oxford, England, 1990, p. 29.

77. Seneca, Lucius Annaeus, "On Providence," in *The Stoic Philosophy of Seneca: Essays and Letters*, W.W. Norton, New York, p. 36.

78. Cicero, Marcu Tullius, "On Old Age," in *Cicero: Selected Works*, p. 233.

79. Ibid., p. 232.

80. Montaigne, Michel de, "That the taste of good and evil depends in large part on the opinion we have of them," *The Complete Essays of Montaigne*, I, 14, p. 38.

81. Ibid.

82. Montaigne, Michel de, "Of the resemblance of children to their fathers," *The Complete Essays of Montaigne*, II, 37, p. 577.

83. Seneca, Lucius Annaeus, "Letter on Suicide," *The Stoic Philosophy of Seneca*, pp. 202-203.

84. Plato, *Phaedo*, in Edith Hamilton and Huntington Cairns, eds., *Plato: The Collected Dialogues*, 61b.

85. Montaigne, Michel de, "A Custom of Cea," *The Complete Essays of Montaigne*, II, 3, p. 253.

86. Ibid.

87. Ibid., p. 255.

88. Plato, *Phaedo*, in Edith Hamilton and Huntington Cairns, eds., *Plato: The Collected Dialogues*, 69b, c.

89. Ibid., *Phaedo*, 113d.

90. Cicero, Marcus Tullius, "On Old Age," in *Cicero: Selected Works*, p. 247.

91. Ibid., pp. 246-247.

92. Cicero, Marcus Tullius, *Tusculan Disputations*, Loeb Classical Library, Harvard University Press, Cambridge, Mass., 2001, pp. 117-119.

93. Seneca, Lucius Annaeus, "Letter 102: On Immortality," *The Stoic Philosophy of Seneca: Essays and Letters*, W.W. Norton, New York, pp. 253-254.

94. Seneca, Lucius Annaeus, "To Marcia on Consolation," *Seneca*: *Moral Essays*, Loeb Classical Library, Harvard University Press, Cambridge, Mass., Vol. II, xxvi, 4-6, p. 95.

95. Gray, Thomas, "Elegy Written in a Country Churchyard," in Kerrigan, Michael, *The History of Death: Burial Customs and Funeral Rites, from the Ancient World to Modern Times*, The Lyons Press, Guilford, Conn., 2007, p. 140.

96. Montaigne, Michel de, "That to philosophize is to learn to die," *The Complete Essays of Montaigne*, p. 67.

97. Plato, *Apology*, in *The Last Days of Socrates*. Penguin Classics, Baltimore, Maryland, 1969, 42a, p. 76.

PART TWO
A PHILOSOPHER'S VIEW OF HEAVEN

CHAPTER 5. IN THE BEGINNING

98. Plato, *Phaedo*, in *The Last Days of Socrates*, Penguin Classics, Baltimore, Maryland, 1969, 61b, p. 104.

99. Alighiera, Dante, *The Paradiso*, Penguin-Putnam, Inc., New York, 1970, p. ix.

100. Plato, *Phaedo*, in *The Last Days of Socrates*, 84d-86b, p. 139.

101. Ecclesiastes, 9, 10.

102. Seneca, Lucius Annaeus, "Letter on Immortality," in *The Stoic Philosophy of Seneca*, p. 7.

103. Shakespeare, William, *Hamlet*, Act I, Scene 5, 159-167.

104. Montaigne, Michel de, "It is folly to measure the true and the false by our own capacity," *The Complete Essays of Montaigne*, I, 27, pp. 132-133.

105. Chesterton, G.K., *Tremendous Trifles*, Dover Publications, New York, 2007, p. 7.

106. Chesterton, G.K., *Heretics*, Dover Publications, 2006, p. 31.

107. Pascal, Blaise, *Pensees and Other Writings*, Oxford University Press, 2008, #444, p. 104.

108. Montaigne, Michel de, "It is folly to measure the true and the false by our own capacity," *The Complete Essays of Montaigne*, I, 27, p. 134.

109. Rousseau, Jean-Jacques, *The Creed of a Priest of Savoy*, Frederick Ungar Publishing Co., New York, 1957, p. 29.

110. Kant, Immanuel, *Religion Within the Limits of Reason Alone*, trans., Theodore Greene, Harper and Row, New York, 1960, pp. 44-45.

111. Ibid., lxv.

112. Ibid., lix.

113. Newton, Isaac, quoted in Hawking, Stephen, *On the Shoulders of Giants*, Running Press, 2003, p. 731.

114. Kant, Immanuel, *The Critique of Judgment*, quoted in Kant, *Religion Within the Limits of Reason Alone*, pp. xlv-xlvi.

115. Ibid.

116. Leibniz, Gottfried, quoted in *A Companion to Philosophy of Religion*, eds., Quinn, Philip L. and Tallaferro, Charles, Blackwell Publishing, Malden, Mass., 1999, p. 334.

117. Leibniz, Gottfried, "On the Origination of Things," quoted in Swinburne, Richard, *The Existence of God*, Oxford University Press, 2004, p. 143.

118. Cicero, Marcus Tullius, The Nature of the Gods, Penguin Books, London, England, 1988, Book I, 12, p. 74.

119. Hume, David, *Writings on Religion*, ed., Anthony Flew, Open Court, Illinois, 1992, p. 56.

CHAPTER 6. PERFECT JUSTICE

120. Alighieri, Dante, *The Paradiso*, Canto XVIII, 76-79, trans., John Ciardi, Penguin-Putnam, Inc., New York, 1970, p. 207. Also Canto XXII, 22-23, p. 246.

121. Milton, John Milton, *Paradise Lost*, New American Library, New York, 1961, Book VI, 660, p. 185.

122. Plutarch, "On the Delay of Divine Vengeance," in *Plutarch's Moralia*, Vol. VII, 564, p. 277, Loeb Classical Library, Harvard University Press, Cambridge, Mass., 1996, xxvi, 4, p. 95.

123. I Corinthians, 13, 12.

124. Seneca, Lucius Annaeus, "To Marcia on Consolation," in *Seneca: Moral Essays*, xxvi, 4, p. 95.

125. Alighieri, Dante, *The Paradiso*, Canto XXII, 22-24, p. 246.

126. Milton, John, *Paradise Lost*, New American Library, New York, 1961, Book VIII, 615-630, pp. 231-232.

127. Plato, *The Laws*, in Edith Hamilton and Huntington Cairns, eds., *Plato: The Collected Dialogues*, Book IX, 870.

128. Plato, *The Laws*, Book IX, 872-73.

129. Greene, Brian, *The Elegant Universe*, Vintage Books, New York, p. 169.

130. Kant, Immanuel, *Religion Within the Limits of Reason Alone*, trans., Theodore Greene, Harper and Row, New York, 1960, p. lix.

131. Plutarch, "How to Profit by One's Enemies," in *Moralia*, VII, Harvard University Press, Cambridge, Mass., 1959, p. 5.

132. Plato, *Apology*, in *The Last Days of Socrates*, 41b-42a, pp. 75-76.

133. Nietzsche, Friedrich, *The Gay Science*, trans., Walter Kaufman, Vintage Books, New York, 1974, Book III, 249, p. 215.

134. Ibid., 620d.

135. Plato, *Phaedo*, in *The Last Days of Socrates*, 107c-108b, p. 171.

CHAPTER 7. TRUTH, GOODNESS, AND BEAUTY

136. Nietzsche, Friedrich, "Attempt at Self-Criticism," in *The Birth of Tragedy and The Case of Wagner*, trans., Walter Kaufman, Vintage Books, New York, 1967, p. 22.

137. Plato, *The Laws*, in Edith Hamilton and Huntington Cairns, eds., *Plato: The Collected Dialogues*, 803b-c.

138. Alighieri, Dante, *The Paradiso*, Canto XXII, 9, trans., John Ciardi, Penguin-Putnam, Inc., New York, 1970, p. 246.

139. Alighieri, Dante, *The Purgatorio*, New American Library, New York, 2001, Canto XV, 74-75, p. 163.

140. Santayana, George, *The Sense of Beauty*, Dover Publications, Inc., New York, 1955, pp. 19-20.

141. Lewis, C.S., *The Problem of Pain*, HarperCollins, San Francisco, Calif., 1996, pp. 151-152, pp. 155-156.

142. lutarch, "On the Delay of the Divine Vengeance," in *Moralia*, VII, Harvard University Press, Cambridge, Mass., 1959, 556, p. 227.

143. Nietzsche, Friedrich, "On the Uses and Disadvantages of History for Life," in *Untimely Meditations*, Daniel Breazeale, ed., Cambridge University Press, Cambridge, Mass., 1999, p. 62.

144. Aristotle, *Nicomachean Ethics*, Penguin Books, 1982, Book I, x, 1100a20-69, p. 85.

145. Ibid. Book I, x, 1100a10-34.

146. Ibid., Book X, vii, 1177b33-1178a21, p. 331.

147. Ibid., Book I, xi, 1101a20-69, p. 85.

CHAPTER 8. A SENSIBLE AFTERLIFE

148. Jefferson, Thomas, Letter to William Short, May 5, 1816.

149. I can't help but cite these passages from the Bible: Matthew 21:21, Mark 11:23, Luke 10:19, John 14:12.

150. Kant, Immanuel, *Groundwork of a Metaphysics of Morals*, trans., H.J. Paton, Harper & Row, Publishers, New York, 1964, Ch. 1, p. 61.

151. Matthew, 5, 27-28.

152. Psalm lxxviii, 25.

153. Milton, John, *Paradise Lost*, Book V, 630-638

154. Ibid., Book III, 135, p. 94.

155. Augustine of Hippo, quoted in Thomas Aquinas, *Summa Theologica*, Vol. V., Question 70, First Article, p. 2825, Christian Classics, Westminster, Maryland, 1981.

156. Lewis, C.S., *Miracles*, HarperOne, New York, 1996, p. 261.

157. Ibid., p. 261.

158. Matthew, 22:23-30.

159. Nietzsche, Friedrich, *The Gay Science*, Vintage Books, New York, 1974, Book IV, 337.

160. Aristotle, *Nicomachean Ethics*, Book X, viii, 1178b7-29, p. 333.

161. Nussbaum, Martha, *The Theory of Desire: Theory and Practice in Hellenistic Ethics*, Princeton University Press, Princeton, New Jersey, 1994, p. 226.

162. Ibid., p. 227.

163. Plato, *Phaedo*, in *The Last Days of Socrates*, Penguin Classics, Baltimore, Maryland, 1969, p. 178.